W9-AQB-612

HF 5823 .V53 1995

Vitale, Joseph G.

AMA complete guide to small
  business advertising

DATE DU

AMA Complete Guide to
SMALL
BUSINESS
ADVERTISING

Joe Vitale

Printed on recyclable paper

NTC Business Books
a division of *NTC Publishing Group* • Lincolnwood, Illinois USA

Library of Congress Cataloging-in-Publication Data

Vitale, Joseph G.
   AMA complete guide to small business advertising / Joe Vitale.
     p.   cm.
   Includes bibliographical references and index.
   1. Advertising—Handbooks, manuals, etc. 2. Small business—
   Management—Handbooks, manuals, etc. I. title.
  HF5823.V53 1995
  659.2'81—dc20   94–14170
                                          CIP

Published in conjunction with the American Marketing Association,
250 South Wacker Drive, Chicago, Illinois 60606.

Published by NTC Business Books, a division of NTC Publishing Group.
© 1995 by NTC Publishing Group, 4255 West Touhy Avenue,
Lincolnwood (Chicago), Illinois 60646-1975 U.S.A.
Manufactured in the United States of America.

4 5 6 7 8 9 BC 9 8 7 6 5 4 3 2 1

Dedication

This book is dedicated to the *We Sell—Or Else!* spirit of advertising broadcast by the pioneers and legends of the business: Bruce Barton, Helen Woodward, John Caples, David Ogilvy, Claude Hopkins, Maxwell Sackheim, Robert Collier, Charles Austin Bates, and John E. Kennedy.

Table of Contents

Chapter Seven
How to Use Testimonials, Guarantees, and Coupons — 87

Chapter Eight
How to Create Explosive Direct Mail — 111

Chapter Nine
How to Make Classified Ads Work for You — 127

Acknowledgments

Many people helped me rewrite and edit this book. My list of supporters include: Mark Weisser, Louise Dewey, Bob Bly, Greg Manning, Scott Hammaker, Chris Ryan, Jim King, Allison Owen, Connie Schmidt, Don Massey, Sandra Stokes, Tina Nokes, and Murray Raphel. Thanks also to my editors, Anne Knudsen and Betsy Lancefield, and my wife, Marian.

Foreword

Did you know that small businesses in the U.S. . . .

- Provided more than 90 percent of all the new jobs in the past ten years
- Employ 65 percent of the private work force
- File about 20 million business tax returns every year—more than the population of every state except California
- Contribute more to their communities in terms of cash and in-kind services on a per-employee basis than their larger corporate cousins

To paraphrase Winston Churchill, "never has so much been done by so few for so many."

Independent business people are Jacks (or Jacquelines) of all trades. They not only buy and sell—their duties range from picking up the paper on the floor (that no one else ever sees) to checking on why strange cars are in the parking lot to calling the plumber for the leak that's now three inches high in the back room to screaming at the supplier on the phone for merchandise promised last week, advertised today but never received.

They are entrepreneurial and, for the most part, learn by doing.

When you speak to them about how to advertise their business, their look is impatient, uninterested and says "I'm worried about the fact that three cashiers called in sick this morning and I don't have anybody to handle the front end."

They set aside the least amount of time for the most important salesperson they have: their advertising.

And so they learn what works best by trying. And succeeding. Or failing. And trying to remember a few weeks later what worked and what didn't work. And, most important . . . *why?*

We spent forty years in retailing, starting with a 600-square-foot baby shop that grew to almost a block-long shopping area in Atlantic City called Gordon's Alley with 40 shops, restaurants and offices.

We knew the importance and value of advertising but we didn't know how to do it. We were at the mercy of the salesperson from the local (check one) radio, newspaper, TV and yellow pages who would try to persuade us that not spending money advertising with them might mean a notice of our business in the obituary pages of next year's financial newspapers. We would need to spend money with them to make sure we would not have to take down our neon, fold up our retailing tent and silently fade away. . . .

We would often wonder why there was no book, text, instruction manual, tips, advice . . . something that would give us a clue as to what worked and what didn't in advertising . . . and why.

Yes, we were familiar with the time-honored John Wanamaker phrase that "half the money I spend in advertising is wasted. I only wish I knew which half."

Hey, we were interested in the half that WORKED. Would somebody tell us the secrets, the direction, the magic formulas?

Sorry, not available in the local library.

Sorry, not willing to be supplied by other retailers who worried if someone spent more money with you they would spend less money with them.

Sorry, nowhere to turn.

But now. . . .(Offstage sound of trumpets and loud huzzahs!)
The answers are in your hands.

Joe Vitale's book is an invaluable guide to the small business-man or -woman. You can pick it up and read as much as you want. You can start at the beginning, middle or end. You will understand, learn, find out the Do's and Don'ts and how they can be used in your business.

I only had one thought when I finished reading:

"Joe . . . where were you forty years ago when I needed you?!"

Murray Raphel
Atlantic City, N.J.

Introduction

Advertising is one of the most costly, necessary and yet unpredictable expenses of any business. Without it a business has little chance of surviving. With it—if the advertising is done poorly (and most of the time it is)—a business can still fail.

Part of the reason for this is that most people don't understand the fundamental principles of advertising. Even ad agencies and respected copywriters don't seem to know the basics.

One of the complaints of advertising legend David Ogilvy is that so few people in advertising ever read anything about the business. I have. In fact, I've been obsessed about obtaining every book on the subject, even if the titles were a hundred years old. I wanted to learn everything about the subject so I could distill the information into principles that would work for anyone's business—large or small, no matter what the business—and work in today's world.

I've also been obsessed with interviewing the experts and double-checking my facts. I may be accused of oversimplifying the information and not revealing all of my sources, but one raw, priceless fact remains:

These ideas work!

Now, maybe for the first time in history, there is one book you can refer to for the help you need in creating ads or commercials that will help you sell your small business product or service. Thanks to NTC Business Books and the American Marketing Association, you are now holding that book.

This is not a book of rules, but a book of ideas, suggestions and principles. Bill Bernback, another of the legends of the ad business, once wrote: "Principles endure, formulas don't. You must get attention to your ad. This is a principle that will always be true; *how* you get attention is a subtle, ever-changing thing."

May these principles, your own imagination and hard work make you and your small business prosperous. They've worked for me and my clients. Now it's your turn to achieve success.

Joe Vitale
Houston

Chapter One

Why *You* Must Advertise

Imagine a couple who open their own grocery store. *How do they get customers?*

Imagine an entrepreneur with a hot idea or an inventor with a new product. *How do they let the world know about their creations?*

And imagine an office supply store being opened right down the street from three other office supply stores. *How does the new one get any business?*

"Any fool can make soap," said Thomas Barratt of Pears' soap, which was once a very small business. "It takes a clever man to sell it."

There may not be much difference between your product or service—your "soap"—and your competition's. And it is advertising that decides who wins in the marketplace. If your competition advertises and you do not, they will probably get more business than you. Why? Because without advertising, no one will know you exist. Or if they do know, they may not know why they should buy from you rather than your competition. If there is a difference between your "soap" and your competition's, how will the public know—*unless you tell them?*

Three Advertising Successes

Have you ever heard of Campbell's Soup, Coca–Cola, or Ivory Soap? Of course you have. All three were top sellers in 1923 *and* in 1993. That's seventy *years* of consistent success. That means they survived the Great Depression, several recessions, World War II, and several national panics.

And all three started like you: from scratch. All three began as small businesses. They owe their success to two traits: a good product and effective advertising. No matter what was happening, those three major league companies continued to promote their wares.

"In good times people want to advertise," said Bruce Barton, a founder of BBDO, one of the largest advertising agencies in the world (which began as a small business in 1919). "In bad times they have to." In today's fierce business arena, over 80 percent of all new businesses go out of business within three years. Though some of them are poorly managed or are selling products or services few want, the vast majority would succeed *if* they effectively advertised.

Advertising Defined

In small businesses people tend to confuse marketing, public relations, and advertising. Though the three overlap in their functions, they each have a separate role to play in the success of your business.

Marketing

Marketing is how you get your product or service to people. Choosing to put a store on a particular corner is a marketing decision. Choosing to advertise is a marketing decision, too. Marketing does not persuade people to buy your goods, but it does make it easier for them to buy. Marketing puts your product or service out there in the marketplace.

Public Relations

Public relations is any attempt to influence public opinion in the direction of your small business. Sending out a news release about your business, for example, is a public relations attempt to get favorable publicity for your enterprise. Public relations is not controllable because you never know if your release will be printed, or when. And though publicity can create a wonderful image for you (or backfire and destroy your image), it doesn't motivate anyone to buy, or even tell them how to reach you. Public relations tells people about your product or service.

Advertising

Advertising is a paid attempt to sell a product or service to a particular group of people. When you buy space in the local newspaper and fill it with your own words, you are advertising. If you do it right, you can reach prospective customers, convince them to buy, and tell them how to do what you want. Advertising persuades people to *buy* your product or service.

David Ogilvy (whose small advertising business is now an empire) wrote in *Ogilvy On Advertising*

> McGraw–Hill tells us that the average salesman's call costs $178.00, a letter $6.63 and a phone call $6.35, while you can reach a prospect through advertising for only 17 cents.

That was in 1985. Today, the figures are much higher. One study claims that reaching a prospect in person can cost $500.00 or more. Advertising is still one of the most cost effective ways for reaching your potential buyers.

You want to do more than reach a prospect, of course. You want to reach and urge that person to *buy*. To be effective, advertising must:

1. **Tell people you exist.**

   It can create an image for yourself and your company. And it's faster than "word of mouth" advertising, which you can influence but not control. In other words, you know your product is great and your family knows it. But advertising can help tell the rest of the world about it.

2. **Tell people what you sell.**

   Educating the public has long been one of advertising's strong points. You never knew "7-Up" (which began as a small business) could settle an upset stomach until their advertising told you. Whether you're a painter or a plumber, or any other small business, advertising can help inform people about what you do or sell.

3. **Tell people where you are.**

   If you open a restaurant or a dress shop, you have to tell people where it is located. You can't rely on people accidentally driving by your business. If you want them to know where you are located, advertising can tell them.

4. **Tell people why they should buy from you.**
   If you open a beauty shop on the same street where another beauty shop already exists, how are you going to get people in *your* door? Advertising can tell people why they should buy from you rather than your competitors.

Direct Response Advertising

The purpose of this book is to give you the proven guidelines for creating ads that get results. In other words, rather than trying to create an image for your business, your ads should try to make immediate sales. The technical term for this is *direct response advertising.* When you do this right, you also create an image.

A friend in Nashville told me that a local radio station uses a particular ad to create the image that their station is fun. I asked if that ad got them more listeners. My friend didn't know. And that's the problem with image advertising. It isn't measurable and it seldom gets the results you want.

Direct response ads, however, are designed to get a direct and immediate response. They are designed *to sell.* Since so few small businesses advertise, and so few that do have any idea what they are doing, just having this book in your hands will give you an edge over the competition. But *using* this book will determine how well you do in the marketplace. So let's get started!

 Action Point

Your first assignment is to complete **Worksheet 1.** This will give you a current picture of your business. Answer each question as specifically as you can.

Worksheet 1

Do You Qualify for Success?

1. Do you have a product or service of real value?
Unless you tap into a pre-existing universal need (love, sex, security, power, etc.), you will have a tough time selling your wares.

What are you selling? _____

_____

_____

_____

2. Does a specific group of people want it?
Unless a group of people is targeted, any advertising you do will be too scattered to get results. You're *not* selling to "everybody."

Who are you selling to? _____

_____

_____

_____

3. Do you regularly let these people know you exist?
You have to constantly advertise your product or service to the group most interested in buying.

Are you currently advertising? _____

_____

_____

_____

4. Does your offer beat the competition's offer?

If you are not better or cheaper or more fully guaranteed, why buy from you? People are spending money all the time. If they are not buying from you, they are buying from someone else.

What is unique about your offer? _____

_____

_____

_____

5. Are you giving something away?

You have to give to get. Are you giving away a free booklet or free consultation or a discount or some other incentive?

What are you giving to people? _____

_____

_____

_____

6. Are your advertisements irresistible selling pieces?

Creative ads win awards but often lose sales. The war cry of your advertising should be "We sell—*or else!*"

Do your ads get results? _____

_____

_____

_____

Chapter Two

Three Proven Advertising Formulas Any Business Can Use

Read this information . . .	. . . complete this Action Point
AIDA	
PAPA	
Six Keys for Creating Ads	Worksheet 2: Three Formulas for Your Business Ads

Many small businesses are convinced they need to advertise. Look in any local newspaper and you will see ads for everything from dental work to shoe stores. But most of those ads are not getting *any* results. They may be cute, or clever, or creative. But they do not sell!

It is not enough for you to run an ad that says "Lawnmowers Repaired Here." It is not enough for you to put your phone number in bold type and say "We give great service!" It is not enough for you to say "John Smith Accountants are the best." You want results—you want sales. The best way to make that happen is to create advertising that is effective. Most small businesses are failing in this area. Yet with the help of some tried and proven formulas, they could easily create advertising that does what all good advertising should do: *Sell!*

AIDA

The most famous and reliable advertising formula of all is *AIDA*. It is probably well over a hundred years old. AIDA means: Attention, Interest, Desire, Action. Though no one has been given credit for developing this formula, it was probably from the mind of John E. Kennedy, the ex-Canadian policeman who, around 1905, gave advertising a definition never since improved: "Advertising is salesmanship in print."

Attention

If you do not get the attention of your potential customers and clients, they will not read your ad. The two best ways of grabbing attention are with a *headline* and an *illustration*. Both will be discussed in detail later. For now, realize that a headline can capture the eye of your audience, stop them, and urge them to read your sales message. An illustration can do the same thing. Combined effectively, they can create an irresistible ad.

The very first thing you want your ad to do is get their **attention.** If you do not have that, what good is anything else in your ad? Nobody will see it!

Interest

Now that you have their attention, what are you going to do with it? Your ad needs to generate interest in your product or service. Writing copy that is persuasive and compelling will be covered later. For now you should begin to realize that an ad has to do many things. Even if you somehow manage to get people's attention, you have to offer something interesting or you will lose that hard-earned attention immediately. Said another way, why should people read your ad? What is in it for them? You have to interest them to hold them.

Desire

You have their attention and you are holding their interest. Now what? You have to generate enthusiasm for your product or service. You have to make these readers desire, want, even *drool* for your offer. Again, we will explore how to do this later. For now, realize that an ad has to walk people up several rungs of a ladder before they get to the point where they are ready to buy. In this step you want to get readers excited.

Action

If you managed to get people to read your ad, what do you want them to do next? You want them to buy. Or call. Or visit. Or mail in a coupon. You want them to take *action*. You want them to do something—else why even run the ad? The last step in this formula is encouraging and motivating people to make a move in your favor.

AIDA is one of the most powerful advertising formulas throughout modern advertising history. With it you can create ads that will stand out, get read, and bring in the results you want. But in addition to AIDA, there are other formulas you can begin to work with immediately.

PAPA

The second formula for successful ads is PAPA. PAPA translates into Promise, Amplify, Proof, and Action. It is another one of those proven, time-honored formulas that have been around for several decades.

Promise

Your ad should begin with a promise to deliver an important benefit. In other words, your headline should offer (promise) something the reader is looking for. If your readers have been wanting to play a musical instrument, "How to Play the Harmonica—Instantly!" is a promise that would appeal to them.

Amplify

Now you need to explain all the benefits your service will give. Give the details about your product or service. Enlarge on your promise. For example, if you own a car repair service, spell out exactly what you do or what types of cars you specialize in repairing. Give some details. Do you have a free loaner car program? Say so.

Proof

You need to prove what you say. People are not fools and they are very skeptical. In this step you can use testimonials from satisfied customers, show the product in use in your illustration, and/or offer a strong guarantee.

Action

This is the same as in the AIDA formula. Everything in your ad should be strategically designed to get readers to *act* and to act *now*.

Before getting into more detail with each of these steps, now you should just begin thinking of what it takes to create an effective ad for *your* small business.

Six Keys for Creating Ads

These six key points make up my own formula for creating ads. AIDA and PAPA are a great starting point; this additional list provides even more help in creating powerful and effective ads.

Appropriate Attention

You do not want to write an ad that just gets attention. You want to get *appropriate* attention. Not everyone who reads the newspaper is a likely candidate for your business, and certainly no one buys a paper to read your ad. You do not need everyone's attention. What you do need is the attention of the people most likely to be interested in what you have to offer.

This is why personalized headlines work well. If your audience is owners of Volkswagens, a possible opening for your ad could be "Attention—VW Owners!" You do not need to grab the ear of Ford or Chevy owners, or anyone else. What you want is a specific audience. To get this you need an illustration and a headline that gets you the appropriate attention of your target audience.

Rouse Interest with Emotion

You do not want your ad to list facts and features like a product spec sheet. You want your ad to *excite* people. You want to arouse their interest, their curiosity, and their desires. The best way to do this is by touching their emotions. Buying decisions are usually made by emotions and then justified by logic. Your ad needs to arouse interest with emotional appeals. While there is an art to doing this, it can be done for any small business.

For example, a jewelry store can advertise their new rings by saying something bland like "New Rings for Sale!" or something much more engaging like "How to Fall in Love Again!"

Prove Claims

People know you paid for the ad, designed the ad, and approved the ad. They are not going to believe anything you say unless you can prove your claims in the ad. You need to run testimonials, excerpts from reviews when possible, and anything else you can think of to lend credibility to your ad. Since we live in the age of skepticism, you must overcome buyer resistance by proving your claims. If your product is the fastest, who says so besides you? If your product can do the impossible, how can you prove it to me?

Guarantee

If you do not guarantee what you do or offer, forget running an ad. People work hard for their money and will not part with it if there is even a wisp of doubt in their minds. Wipe out all doubt by fully guaranteeing what you do. The stronger the guarantee, the better.

One of the most unusual guarantees I ever read was for a book promising to help you find the mate of your dreams. The guarantee was something like, "Use the ideas in this book for three years. If you haven't married the person of your dreams by then, we'll give you your money back!" The guarantee helped sell thousands of books. And as far as I know, no one ever asked for their money back.

Call for Action

You have to tell people what to do before they will do it. If you want them to call you, *tell* them to call you. If you want them to clip out a coupon, *tell* them exactly what to do and how to do it and even when to do it. Spell it out. If you do not instruct them and ask them, they will not do it.

"Return this coupon by October 15th for a *free* surprise gift!" is one example of a call for action. So is "Just call this toll-free number *now!*"

Powerful Statement

Sales letters often end with a postscript that contains a highlighted benefit. It is not an afterthought but a strategically placed sales message. People often read the PS first, last, and recall it the longest. Because the PS is so potent, I have renamed it *powerful statement.*

You can use a PS in your ads, too. After you have covered all the above steps, you can add a PS that includes another powerful reason for buying or calling you. An example might be, "PS—Call today and receive a one hour massage *free!*"

These three formulas for writing effective ads—AIDA, PAPA, and my own six keys—can help you create advertising up to 90 percent more effective than your competitors. While advertising agencies often break the rules and still achieve results, as a small business on a tight budget you cannot afford to take unnecessary risks. Pick one of the above formulas whenever you need to write an ad, follow it, and you will create advertising that works.

After you have completed this book, look at the ads in your local papers. You will see that nearly all of them are done by business owners who think people are sitting around with nothing better to do than read their ads. Combine your knowledge of the three formulas with the three most powerful types of ads in the next chapter, and your competition will start worrying about their survival.

 ## *Action Point*

Take your business or service and begin to formulate an ad for it. For practice, take each of the three formulas and work through their points to create a draft ad on **Worksheet 2.** Then take the formula that worked best for you and fine-tune that draft into an ad.

Worksheet 2

Three Formulas for Your Business Ads

1. AIDA

    a. <u>Attention</u>. What can your ad say, or how can you illustrate your ad, to get the attention of readers? What headline will work best?

    _____
    _____

    b. <u>Interest</u>. What can you say to interest your readers? You managed to get their attention. Why should they keep reading? Remember to think of what your readers will get.

    _____
    _____

    c. <u>Desire</u>. How can you make your readers even more excited about your business? What is unique and special about your offer?

    _____
    _____

    d. <u>Action</u>. What do you want people to do? Call? Write? FAX? Visit? Spell it out. Tell people exactly what they need to do and why they should do it right now.

    _____
    _____

2. PAPA

    a. <u>Promise</u>.

    _____
    _____
    _____

    b. <u>Amplify</u>.

    _____
    _____
    _____

c. Proof.

_____
_____
_____

d. Action.

_____
_____
_____
_____

3. Six keys for creating ads

   a. Appropriate attention.

   _____
   _____

   b. Rouse interest with emotion.

   _____
   _____
   _____

   c. Prove claims.

   _____
   _____

   d. Guarantee.

   _____
   _____
   _____

   e. Call for action.

   _____
   _____
   _____

   f. Powerful statement.

   _____
   _____
   _____

4. Take the formula that works best for you and write an ad with that information here.

_____

_____

_____

_____

_____

_____

Chapter Three

The Three Most Powerful Types of Ads

Read this information . . .	. . . complete this Action Point
Open Letter	
Classic DR	
Advertorial	Worksheet 3: Three Formulas for Your Business Ads

In any small business it is wise to learn from previous successes, whether those successes are yours or your competitors'. This is the "copy cat" principle and it is done frequently in the world of advertising. Find out what has worked before for someone in a business similar to yours, and copy their formula.

There are three types of ads that work well for small business. For the sake of simplicity, I will label them

1. Open Letter
2. Classic DR
3. Advertorial

Let's look at each one and see how you can use them as a model or blueprint for your own advertisements.

Open Letter

The *open letter* ad looks like a letter. It begins with a "Dear reader" or "Dear car buyer" or "Dear friend" or other type of warm salutation, and reads like a very personal letter from someone, usually the owner of a business.

Because this ad does not look like an ad, it gets attention. Because this structure looks very personal, it gets read. Because it is open (not in an envelope but actually printed in a newspaper or magazine for all to see), it compels people to see what it says. It is like a postcard in the sense that it is personal, specific, and too public to resist reading.

All the elements of a good ad must still be in this format, of course. Without attention, interest, desire, and action, people might read your ad but they will not do anything because of it. But how those elements are woven into this form are more subtle.

For example, let us assume you want to run an open letter ad in a Houston paper. One way to write a headline is to say, "An open letter to readers of *The Houston Chronicle*." That is a headline that will get attention. You can run any other type of sub-headline under that, if you want, to help further propel people into actually reading the ad.

Or, if you own a car washing service, you might run your ad with a headline such as, "An open letter to anyone with a dirty car." If you are a barber, it could be "An open letter to anyone who ever needs a haircut." The variety of headlines you can use is enormous. Simply look at the people who use your service, and write an open letter headline tailor-made for them.

What you are doing with this type of ad is writing a powerful and persuasive letter and then running it as an ad. **Exhibit 3.1,** an ad with the headline "An open letter to the readers of *The New*

Exhibit 3.1.
Open letter
ad

An open letter to the readers of The New York Times

Norman Cousins
Two Dag Hammarskjold Plaza   New York, New York 10017

My purpose in writing is to tell you that my colleagues and I have decided to launch a new magazine. The magazine will be published every two weeks. It will be called *World Review*.

Ever since I resigned from the Saturday Review, for reasons you may know about, I have been thinking and dreaming about the possibility of starting a magazine that, quite literally, would belong to its readers and editors.

This has never been done before. Usually, new magazines call for a prodigious investment. The reason for this is the traditional way a magazine operates. Magazines and newspapers are the only products sold to the consumer at less than the cost of manufacture. Advertising is expected to make up the difference. What compounds this problem is that the standard way of building a subscription list is through cut-rate introductory offers.

On a new magazine, the subscription list generally consists almost entirely of cut-rate introductory offers. This is why massive outside investment has usually been necessary to see a magazine through to the point where introductory-offer readers can be graduated to full-rate subscribers. Outside investment frequently means outside control—and this is something we want to avoid if we possibly can.

My hope, therefore, is that we can find enough readers willing to take a chance on us by becoming long-term subscribers from the very outset. This would make it unnecessary to seek outside financing. It would also put the reader where he should rightfully be—in a position of ultimate authority.

We decided to put these hopes to the test. I am delighted to say that the first responses to our testing have been favorable beyond even our most extravagant expectations. As a result, we are scheduling our first issue for late in the spring.

What about the magazine itself?

We believe that a magazine is essentially a reading, rather than a viewing, experience. In this sense, we will publish for a readership rather than a flippership.

The new magazine will be concerned with ideas and the arts. Our arena, however, will be the world. We will do more than report on books, plays, movies, music and the arts in just the United States alone. We will attempt to review and report on cultural events on a world scale—cultural being defined in its broadest sense.

We will write about the human condition at a time when the ability of human intelligence to meet its problems is being tested as never before. Our hope is to see the world as the astronauts saw it—a beautiful wet blue ball with millions of factors in the delicate combination that makes life possible. Our dominant editorial concern, then, will be the proper care of the human habitat—whether that means world peace and everything that is required to bring it about, or world environmental deterioration, or overcrowding, or any of the things that indignify and humiliate human beings.

In this connection, I am pleased to announce that U Thant and Buckminster Fuller have joined the Board of Editors.

We will also give major attention to what we believe will be one of the most compelling issues in the years ahead—the waste of human resources, far more costly than the waste of physical resources.

I think I have said enough to indicate that the new magazine will direct its central editorial energies both to the enjoyment of creative living and to the pursuit of vital ideas. But it would be a mistake, I think, to attempt a full description of the magazine. Magazines are not really invented or created. They evolve. They are the product of creative interaction between the special tastes and enthusiasms and concerns of a few editors, and the tastes and concerns of the readers.

In this way, a magazine takes shape issue by issue and year by year. No single issue can really be expected to tell a reader everything he may want to know about the nature of a magazine, its underlying philosophy, or its capacity for growth. Since it might be misleading to try to tell you exactly what our new magazine will be like, what I have tried to do is to tell you something about our philosophy and our approach—and to seek your help in achieving our aims.

Some specifics: The rates will be $12 for one year; $20 for two years.

For pre-publication Charter subscribers we propose a special three-year rate of $25.

The reason we emphasize three-year subscriptions is that this reduces sharply the astoundingly high cost of processing renewals.

Even more important is the fact that long-term subscriptions will free us to do our main job—which is to try to publish a magazine you will read and respect.

We ask no money now. That can come later. What we do need right now is an expression of your interest.

As I said above, in inviting you to join us in what we hope will be an exciting adventure in ideas, we realize we are asking you to take a chance on us. We have high hopes of justifying that confidence. The process begins with the Charter Subscription form below.

Sincerely,

Norman Cousins

WORLD REVIEW
Two Dag Hammarskjold Plaza
New York, N.Y. 10017

Please enter my subscription and bill me later at the charter rate.
☐ $25 for three years   ☐ $20 for two years
☐ $12 for a one year subscription

Name_____
Address_____
City_____ State_____ Zip_____

York Times," is a classic example of an open letter ad. It ran in *The New York Times* three times and pulled $54,923 worth of subscriptions. Notice how it looks like a letter, even when there is a coupon at the bottom of it.

Classic DR

This type of ad is a textbook *direct response* ad. It is designed to elicit a reply from readers. On the strength of the ad alone, you want people to buy, call, or visit you. You want a direct response.

Typically, a direct response ad has a big, bold, riveting headline at the top of the page, an eye-catching illustration to the left of the headline or in the middle of it, and long body copy broken up with subheads to make reading a breeze. There are testimonials set off in italics so they are easy to find, a guarantee in a box so it leaps off the page, and, on the bottom right-hand side of the page, a coupon or a toll-free number demanding immediate action.

Though this format is a winner, it is seldom used. Some people believe there is too much on the page for anyone to stop and read. Yet the truth is that if people are interested, they will read every word—no matter how many words there are! As long as your ad is targeted to a specific group of people with a clear benefit for them, and it is well written, it will be read.

Others feel this type of ad is too old-fashioned to work. Yet this ad format is the first choice of many experienced mail-order businesses. An ad that tells a complete story in this format gets noticed, gets read, and gets action. This format causes readers to stop and look because they know, maybe unconsciously, that something interesting is being offered. **Exhibit 3.2,** written by Maxwell Sackheim, is one of the most famous ads in history. It ran *40 years!* Note how the powerful headline drags you right into the ad. Also note the testimonials, the intriguing photograph, and the coupon.

Advertorial

Imagine this situation: A friend of yours happens to be a reporter for the local newspaper. She stops by and talks to you about your small business. Because this is a friend, she writes a rave review of you and what you do. She writes it as a solid news story, full

Exhibit 3.2. Direct response ad

Do You Make These Mistakes in English?

Sherwin Cody's remarkable invention has enabled more than 100,000 people to correct their mistakes in English. Only 15 minutes a day required to improve your speech and writing.

MANY persons use such expressions as "Leave them lay there" and "Mary was invited as well as myself." Still others say "between you and I" instead of "between you and me." It is astonishing how often "who" is used for "whom" and how frequently we hear such glaring mispronunciations as "for MID able," "ave NOO," and "KEW pon." Few know whether to spell certain words with one or two "c's" or "m's" or "r's" or with "ie" or "ei," and when to use commas in order to make their meaning absolutely clear. Most persons use only common words—colorless, flat, ordinary. Their speech and their letters are lifeless, monotonous, humdrum.

Why Most People Make Mistakes

What is the reason so many of us are deficient in the use of English and find our careers stunted in consequence? Why is it some cannot spell correctly and others cannot punctuate? Why do so many find themselves at a loss for words to express their meaning adequately? The reason for the deficiency is clear. Sherwin Cody discovered it in scientific tests which he gave thousands of times. *Most persons do not write or speak good English simply because they never formed the habit of doing so.*

What Cody Did at Gary

The formation of any habit comes only from constant practice. Shakespeare, you may be sure, never studied rules. No one who writes and speaks correctly thinks of *rules* when he is doing so.

Here is our mother-tongue, a language that has built up our civilization, and without which we should all still be muttering savages! Yet our schools, by wrong methods, have made it a study to be avoided—the hardest of tasks instead of the most fascinating of games! For years it has been a crying disgrace.

In that point lies the real difference between Sherwin Cody and the schools! Here is an illustration: Some years ago Mr. Cody was invited by the author of the famous Gary System of Education to teach English to all upper-grade pupils in Gary, Indiana. By means of unique practice exercises *Mr. Cody secured more improvement in these pupils in five weeks than previously had been obtained by similar pupils in two years under old methods.* There was no guesswork about these results. They were proved by scientific comparisons. Amazing as this improvement was, more interesting still was the fact that the children were "wild" about the study. It was like playing a game!

The basic principle of Mr. Cody's new method is habit-forming. Anyone can learn to write and speak correctly by constantly using the correct forms. But how is one to know in each case what is correct? Mr. Cody solves this problem in a simple, unique, sensible way.

100% Self-Correcting Device

Suppose he himself were standing forever at your elbow. Every time you mispronounced or misspelled a word, every time you violated correct grammatical usage, every time you used the wrong word to express what you meant, suppose you could hear him whisper: "That is wrong, it should be thus and so." In a short time you would habitually use the correct form and the right words in speaking and writing.

If you continued to make the same mistakes over and over again, each time patiently he would tell you what was right. He would, as it were, be an everlasting mentor beside you—a mentor who would not laugh at you, but who would, on the contrary, support and help you. The 100% Self-Correcting Device does exactly this thing. It is Mr. Cody's silent voice behind you, ready to speak out whenever you commit an error. It finds your mistakes and concentrates on them. You do not need to study anything you already know. There are no rules to memorize.

Only 15 Minutes a Day

Nor is there very much to learn. In Mr. Cody's years of experimenting he brought to light some highly astonishing facts about English.

For instance, statistics show that a list of sixty-nine words (with their repetitions) *make up more than half of all our speech and letter-writing.* Obviously, if one could learn to spell, use, and pronounce these words correctly, one would go far toward eliminating incorrect spelling and pronunciation.

Similarly, Mr. Cody proved that there were no more than one dozen fundamental principles of punctuation. If we mastered these principles, there would be no bugbear of punctuation to handicap us in our writing.

Finally he discovered that twenty-five typical errors in grammar constitute nine-tenths of our everyday mistakes. When one has learned to avoid these twenty-five pitfalls, how readily one can obtain the facility of speech which denotes the person of breeding and education!

When the study of English is made so simple, it becomes clear that progress can be made in a very short time. *No more than fifteen minutes a day is required.* Fifteen minutes, not of study, but of fascinating practice! Mr. Cody's students do their work in any spare moment they can snatch. They do it riding to work or at home. They take fifteen minutes from the time usually spent in profitless reading or amusement. The results really are phenomenal.

Sherwin Cody has placed an excellent command of the English language within the grasp of everyone. Those who take advantage of his method gain something so priceless that it cannot be measured in terms of money. They gain a mark of breeding that cannot be erased as long as they live. They gain a facility in speech that marks them as educated people in whatever society they find themselves. They gain the self-confidence and self-respect which this ability inspires. As for material reward, certainly the importance of good English in the race for success cannot be overestimated. Surely, no one can advance far without it.

FREE — Book on English

It is impossible in this brief review to give more than a suggestion of the range of subjects covered by Mr. Cody's new method and of what his practice exercises consist. But those who are interested can find a detailed description in a fascinating little book called "How You Can Master Good English in 15 Minutes a Day." This is published by the Sherwin Cody School of English in Rochester. It can be had by anyone, free upon request. There is no obligation involved in writing for it. The book is more than a prospectus. Unquestionably, it tells one of the most interesting stories about education in English ever written.

If you are interested in learning more in detail of what Sherwin Cody can do for you, send for the book "How You Can Master Good English in 15 Minutes a Day."

Merely mail the coupon, a letter or postal card for it now. No agent will call. SHERWIN CODY SCHOOL OF ENGLISH, 8811 B. & O. Building, Rochester 4, N. Y.

SHERWIN CODY

of facts and figures and quotes, but without any negative slants. The finished story is a wonderful tribute to your business. That is an *advertorial*—an advertisement–editorial. It is an ad written in a disguised format, looking like a newspaper or magazine feature. Readers are up to 500 times more likely to read an advertorial than a straight ad.

You can run an ad that says "Get a Massage to Heal Your Back" and, if it is done right, you will get some business. But an advertorial on the same subject might have a more "newsy" headline, such as "Massage Found to Relieve Backaches." The story under it would read as if a journalist wrote it who was convinced that massages are the key to health and healing. Because people want news, a story promising information will get noticed and read.

An advertorial (as well as the other formats) should still have all the ingredients of a good ad, of course. The headline should get attention, the body copy should generate interest and desire, and the ending should encourage readers and tell them how to order or buy what was described.

Exhibit 3.3 is an example of an advertorial ad that ran in *Reader's Digest*. Note how it resembles an article that would be published in that magazine. Legendary copywriter John Caples said one test proved that an ad in this format outpulled an ad for the same product set in a different format by 81 percent!

Ads come in all shapes and sizes and formats. But ads that work are often based on proven formats. Put your message in an *open letter* format, a traditional *direct response* form, or make it look like a newspaper feature story with the *advertorial* format, and you will increase the odds for your ad's success. Keep in mind that *any* business can use any of the above ad formats. All you have to do is think about how you can apply the format to your business. And keep in mind that once you have written an ad in any of the formats, you can simply take the existing copy and insert it in one of the other formats.

I once saw an *open letter* ad in a major newspaper selling a tape set. A little later I saw the same ad—word for word—in a major magazine, only this time it was in an *advertorial* format. Not long after that, I ran across a *direct response* ad by the same company— and all of the copy was the same! All they did was restructure their layout to see which format brought in the most orders.

**Exhibit 3.3.
Advertorial
ad**

Action Point

Using **Worksheet 3,** frame three different ads for your business, using each of the formats discussed: open letter, advertorial, and classic DR. You will want to refer to your work on **Worksheet 1** for copy ideas. And remember that your copy can be the same for each format.

Worksheet 3

Three Formats for Your Business Ads

1. An *open letter* for a beauty salon might begin like this: "An open letter to women." The letter itself could be a personal account of why you created your small business (including what is different about it), what women are saying about your service, and so forth. Another angle might be to have the letter come from the perspective of one of your customers who is talking about your salon and encouraging other women to go in for a visit.

   _____

   _____

   _____

   _____

   _____

   _____

   _____

   _____

   _____

   _____

   _____

   _____

   _____

   _____

   _____

   _____

2. A *classic DR* form might begin with this headline: "Does Your Beauty Salon Pass This Test?" You might then have a series of five questions about what to look for in a good salon. Your ad could then go on and talk about your salon, how it passes the test, etc. Another approach would be to begin with a targeted headline, such as "WANTED: Women!" The rest of the ad could explain why women should go to your salon. There could be a coupon at the bottom for a discount, or buy one–get one free make-over, hair cut, etc.

_____
_____
_____
_____
_____
_____
_____
_____
_____
_____
_____
_____
_____
_____
_____
_____

3. An *advertorial* approach might begin: "New Beauty Salon Offers Unique Service." The text itself would be written in a newspaper style about your salon, the people who work there, what customers are saying, and so on. A different view might be to begin with a headline that says, "Local Salon Turns out Movie Stars." Your story could be about your salon's emphasis on making women look glamorous. This would be a very objective yet "rave review" of your business.

_____
_____
_____
_____
_____
_____
_____
_____
_____
_____
_____
_____
_____
_____
_____
_____
_____

Chapter Four

30 Ways to Write a Headline That Stops Customers Dead

Read this information . . .	. . . complete this Action Point
30 Headline Pointers	
How to Test Your Headline	
Proven Headlines	Worksheet 4: Headlines for Your Business Ads

Headlines will make or break your ads. John Caples said a good headline can pull up to *19 times* better results for the same ad. Advertising pioneer James Webb Young said a top headline can bring in as much as *50 percent more* inquiries and sales. Ad genius David Ogilvy said five times more people will read your headlines than will read your whole ad. "We pick out what we wish to read by headlines," wrote Claude Hopkins, arguably the greatest advertising man in history, in his famous book, *Scientific Advertising.*

Often a headline is all a reader will glance at—and I do mean *glance* at—before rushing through the rest of the newspaper or magazine. On average, most people spend only *four seconds* per page! If your headline does not catch, trip, and stop your audience, you have lost them and you have lost a sale!

30 Headline Pointers

Here are 30 surefire ways to create a terrific headline or improve an existing one:

1. Lead with these opening words.

At Last!
Announcing!
New!

Note the hint of excitement and "news" in the above words. Other good opening words include **Introducing** and **Finally.** Legally you can only use the word **New** if your product has been developed or improved within the last six months. If you have just invented a new device, certainly let the world know.

2. Round up your audience.

Plumbers!
Housewives!
Sore Feet?

This type of headline is "calling in" your target audience. If you are selling a book for lawyers, you might open by saying "Attention lawyers!" With this approach you are certain to get the ear of the exact crowd you want.

3. Promise a benefit.

Free from Backache in 10 Minutes!
Buy One Shirt—Get the Second FREE!
Land a Job in 2 Days with New Method!

Benefits are why people buy. Decaffeinated coffee is a feature; "Lets you sleep better" is a benefit. If people have a back problem, they do not want to buy a pill, they want to buy *relief* from their pain. "Free from Backache in 10 Minutes" tells them a cure is available. Sell the relief, not the remedy. Sell the cure, not the prevention.

4. Make it newsworthy.

Major Breakthrough in Car Safety
New Formula Restores Hair
Seven "Lost Secrets" Discovered

People devour news. Reveal the newsworthiness of your product or service and you will get attention. A new product is news. An old product with new uses is news. Arm & Hammer baking soda (which also started as a small business) has been around for decades, but the company keeps thinking of new ways for us to use its product—from brushing our teeth to putting it in the fridge to eliminate odors—and *that's* news.

5. Offer something free.

FREE to Writers!
FREE Report Explains Tax Loopholes
FREE Book on Car Repairs

Your free item has to be appropriate to the audience you are after. It may be free, but if they are not interested in it, they will not write or call you. Also, your free item has to be *really* free—with no catches or conditions—for you to be legally safe. Any small business can create a free item that is relevant.

6. Ask an intriguing question.

What Are the Seven Secrets to Success?
Do You Make These Mistakes in English?
Which Gas Filter Will Boost Your Car's Performance?

Questions are a powerful way to involve readers. But your question has to be an open-ended one that hints of a benefit. If you ask a question that can be easily answered with a "yes" or "no," you run the risk that your readers will not look beyond the question. But if your question is intriguing, it will pull readers into your copy to learn the answer.

7. Lead with a testimonial.

"This is the most powerful weapon I've ever seen!"
(Clint Eastwood)

"These two books made me the wealthiest man alive."
(Malcolm Forbes)

"Here's why my race cars beat all others."
(Mark Weisser)

There is something about quotation marks that captures people's eyes. If your quote is intriguing (as are the fictional ones above), they will force readers to read your copy. (Always use real testimonials from real people and always get their permission first. Chapter Seven will discuss this topic completely.) Anyone who has ever used your product or service can give you a testimonial. And headlines put in quotes will get more attention—dialogue has life, and that attracts people.

8. Create a "how to" headline.

How to Get Your Kids to Listen
How to Tell When Your Car Needs a Tune-Up
How to Win Friends and Influence People

Because people want information, they are easily drawn to "how to" headlines that promise a benefit they are interested in. If you are selling washing machines, you might conjure up the headline "How to Pick the Right Washing Machine for Your Needs." You can add sparkle to virtually any headline by adding the word "how." For example, "I Cut Hair" is a weak headline, but "How I Cut Hair" is more interesting.

9. Quiz your readers.

How Smart Are You? Take This Quiz and See!
What Is Your Networking IQ?
Are You Qualified for Success?

People love quizzes. Use a question headline and then let the body of your ad be a quiz. For the ad to work, of course, it all has to tie in to what you are selling. The ad about your networking IQ, for example, is selling a book called *Power Networking*. If you are running a mechanic's shop, you might ask, "Is Your Car Healthy? Take This Quiz and See!" Your whole attempt is to somehow *involve* readers with your ad. A quiz is one way to do that.

10. Use the words "these" and "why" in your headline.

These Boats Never Sink
Why Our Dogs Cost More
Why These Skis Are Called "Perfect"

When you use the words "these" and "why" in your headline, you tend to create an attention-grabbing statement that will draw readers into the rest of your ad. If you just said, "Our skis are perfect," few would be interested. But when you say, "WHY these skis are called perfect," you generate curiosity—one of the most powerful motivators around. Simply add the word "why" to an existing headline to make it more engaging. "Buy Plumbing Supplies Here" is boring but "Why People Buy Plumbing Supplies Here" is interesting.

11. Use "I" and "me" headlines.

They Laughed When I Sat Down at the Piano—But When I Started to Play!

I Finally Discovered the Secret to Easy Writing!

Everywhere I Stick My Nose I Make Money

First-person headlines will work if they generate enough curiosity and hold a benefit. Everyone interested in playing the piano, for example, will be drawn to the first headline (one of the most successful headlines in history). "You" and "yours" in a headline do not always work because they signal a selling message and people become defensive. However, "I" and "me" in a headline can deliver a selling message in a palatable way. Here's a good example: "I Wanted to Help People So Here's Why I Opened My Own Insurance Agency!"

12. Put your product name in your headline.

How Gymco Vitamins Make Runners Lightning Fast
The Fiskin Ladder Saved My Husband's Life
Thoughtline Helped Me Discover the Secret to Easy Writing

"How to Cure Warts" is good, but "How Vitalism Cures Warts" is better. Since not everyone will stop and read your ad, putting your company name in the headline helps deliver some of your message. But do not make your company name the *focus* of your headline. Instead, write a riveting headline and slip your name in it.

13. Use the word "wanted."

Wanted—Nervous People
Wanted—Safe Men for Dangerous Times
Wanted—Executives Ready for Sudden Profits

"Wanted" is a word loaded with curiosity. Lead with it and people are compelled to find out why you want nervous people (maybe for a seminar on overcoming fear) or why you want executives (maybe to offer them your new investment program). Be sure to ask for the target audience you want. If you are offering something to attorneys, you might write a headline that begins "Wanted—Attorneys."

14. Use the word "breakthrough" in your headline.

A Breakthrough in Alarm Systems
Doctor Offers Breakthrough Hair Loss Formula
Wanted—Attorneys Ready for Breakthrough Success

"Breakthrough" implies news. It suggests that your product or service beats all other existing systems. A similar impact can be obtained with "record breaking" or "revolutionary."

15. Set your headline in upper and lower case.

HEADLINES IN ALL CAPS ARE HARD TO READ
Headlines in Upper and Lower Case Are Easy to Read

Got it?

16. Use as many words as you need.

It Floats!
How Often Do You Hear Yourself Saying: "No, I haven't read it; I've been meaning to!"
Who Else Wants Beautiful Furniture?

Headlines can be long or short. As long as they get the attention of your appropriate audience, arouse curiosity, and encourage people to read your ad, any length goes. You do not want to waste words, of course. But you do not need to limit yourself, either.

17. Feature your offer.

Arrow Shirts at 50% Off
Oil Change Special
Join for Six Months—Get Next Six Months Free

You have to be clear about the uniqueness of what you are selling for this to work. What are you offering that is head and shoulders above your competition? Focus on that.

18. Ask "Who else?"

Who Else Wants to Write a Book?
Who Else Used to Say Singing Was Hard?
Who Else Wants a Fail-Safe Burglar Alarm?

"Who else" is an involving set of words. It suggests that someone else got what you are offering and that it is possible for the reader to achieve or have, too.

19. Use a guarantee.

Guaranteed No-Stains-Ever Rug!

Guaranteed to Go through Ice, Mud, or Snow—or We Pay the Tow!

We live in the age of skepticism. Your ad should always run with a guarantee (more about that later). But if you can say your offer is guaranteed in the headline, it will help to convince readers to look at your entire ad.

20. Admit a weakness.

We're Number Two. We Try Harder.
This Chef Makes Everything Except Salads!

You will gain credibility if you confess you are not perfect. Too many ads claim to be the magic bullet to all your ills. That is not believable. If you say you are *almost* a magic bullet, people will tend to believe the rest of your claims.

21. Focus on positive end results.

Whiter Teeth in 10 Days
35 Pounds Slimmer in 30 Days

Do not paint a negative picture thinking you will make a sale. People buy hopes and dreams. Do not sell "fat loss," instead sell "Perfect Health!" Do not try to scare people into buying toothpaste by yelling "Yellow Teeth Are Ugly," but instead sell the end result people want: "Whiter Teeth!" Again, people buy cures. But be believable. If your headline sounds like a stretch, people will not trust you. "35 pounds slimmer in 30 days" is believable; "35 pounds slimmer overnight" is not.

22. Warn your audience.

WARNING to Doctors!
Warning: Do Your Kids Play This Stereo?
Small Business Owners Be Warned!

You can grab your target audience with a warning to them. A warning promises information and invokes curiosity.

23. Be careful with humor.

Not everyone has a sense of humor, not everyone agrees on what is funny, and few people buy because of a joke. A slogan in advertising is, "People don't buy from clowns." Small businesses that attempt to sell people with their humor usually flop. Why? You are not selling humor, you are selling your product or service. Do you want people to laugh or buy? If you insist on trying humor, try to make the punch line the same as your sales message. Here is an example: "Used Car Prices So Low It Hertz."

24. Make it easy.

Plumbing Problems Cured Easily
Easy Way to Solve Roof Leaks

People want results fast and easy. If you or your product can make their life easier, say so.

25. Be careful with reverse type.

You can use reverse type (white letters on a black background) for your headline but *do not* use reverse type for the rest of your ad. Too much reverse type is far too difficult for people to read. Using it in a headline, however, can increase the number of people who will see the ad.

26. Dramatize the benefit.

Stop Sleeping Like a Sardine! Now Sleep Like a King! "Sound Pillow" Lets You Sleep with Neil Diamond!

People want action. They crave it. Show the excitement your product or service can give by dramatizing the benefits. A headline for large beds that reads "King Size Beds Are Roomy" is boring, but "Stop Sleeping Like a Sardine! Now Sleep Like a King!" is almost impossible to avoid.

27. Use proven cliches.

JUST ARRIVED—New Accounting Method!
ADVICE to Homeowners!
THE TRUTH ABOUT Shoe Repair

David Ogilvy, in *Confessions of an Advertising Man*, lists the following as proven headline cliches:

> Free, New, How To, Suddenly, Now, Announcing, Introducing, It's Here, Just Arrived, Important Development, Improvement, Amazing, Sensational, Remarkable, Revolutionary, Startling, Miracle, Magic, Offer, Quick, Easy, Wanted, Challenge, Advice To, The Truth About, Compare, Bargain, Hurry, Last Chance

Ogilvy also says you can strengthen a headline by adding emotional words, such as: "Darling, Love, Fear, Proud, Friend, and Baby."

28. Reveal a hidden benefit.

"How to Get Enthusiastic Applause—Even a Standing Ovation—Every Time You Speak!"

This headline by Ted Nicholas sold a publication for speakers. One of the hidden or side benefits of reading the publication is learning how to get a standing ovation—something every speaker wants. Try to reveal the hidden benefit in your small business. Ask yourself: "What will people get as a result of using my product or service?"

29. Give reasons.

Three Reasons Why You Should Write a Book
Seven Reasons to Call This Doctor Today
Nine Reasons to Use This Maid Service

Reasons involve readers with your ad. To learn more, they have to read the rest of your copy. The trick to making this work is in targeting your prospects. If you are an accountant, give reasons that tie in to your service. If you are a baker, give reasons why your food is better.

30. Use a before-and-after statement.

The Wrong Way and the Right Way to Buy a Used Car

This is a common way to show how your business can make a difference. If you own a gardening service, you might use a headline that suggests you transform gardens from jungles to parks. What you are doing here is comparing what people have (their problem) with what you can give them (the solution).

How to Test Your Headline

Here is one way to find out if your headline will work—before you spend a cent to run it! Ask yourself: Can this headline be used for any competitor's ad? Imagine placing your headline on a competitor's ad. Will the headline still work?

If your headline will work for them just as well as it would work for you, *change the headline.* Your headline needs to be unique. It needs to show a benefit you offer that no one else does. You are selling your own small business, not your competitor's!

Proven Headlines

Here is a list of winning headlines. Many copywriters read headlines for inspiration when trying to create new headlines. Read over this list to help stimulate your thinking. As you come up with new headlines that you like, write them down. Most advertising people will write several dozen headlines before settling on the handful they really like.

If you find yourself wanting to know more about these headlines, that alone is proof they work. They get your attention, they make you curious, and they compel you to read on and learn more.

Here's a Quick Way to Break Up a Cold

Check the Kind of Body YOU Want

Again She Orders . . . "A Chicken Salad, Please."

Take This 1-Minute Test—of an Amazing New Kind of Shaving Cream

You Never Saw Such Letters as Harry and I Got about Our Pears

New Shampoo Leaves Your Hair Smoother—Easier to Manage

Did You Ever See a "Telegram" from Your Heart?

Imagine Me . . . Holding an Audience Spellbound for 30 Minutes!

This Is Marie Antoinette—Riding to Her Death

Who Else Wants Lighter Cake—in Half the Mixing Time?

Throw Away Your Oars!

Is YOUR Home Picture-Poor?

Guaranteed to Go through Ice, Mud, or Snow—or We Pay the Tow!

Whose Fault When Children Disobey?

How a "Fool Stunt" Made Me a Star Salesman

Doctors Prove 2 out of 3 Women Can Have More Beautiful Skin in 14 Days

Five Familiar Skin Troubles—Which Do You Want to Overcome?

How I Improved My Memory in One Evening

Why Some Foods "Explode" in Your Stomach

When Doctors "Feel Rotten" This Is What They Do

The Secret of Making People Like You

Do You Recognize the Seven Early Warning Signs of High Blood Pressure?

Announcing the New Saturn Cars for 1994

Girls . . . Want Quick Curls?

How Investors Can Save 70% on Commissions This Year

How to Have a Cool, Quiet Bedroom Even on Hot Nights

It Cleans Your Breath When It Cleans Your Teeth

Men Who "know it all" Are Not Invited to Read This Page

Play Guitar in 7 Days or Money Back

If You Are a Careful Driver You Can Save Money on Car Insurance

Reader's Digest Tells Why Filtered Cigarette Smoke Is Better for Your Health

The Deaf Now Hear Whispers

A WARNING to Men Who Want to Be Independent in the Next Five Years

Who Else Wants a Whiter Wash—with No Hard Work?

What's Wrong in this Picture?

Will Your Scalp Stand the "Fingernail Test"?

What Makes a Woman Lovable?

They Thought I Was Crazy to Ship LIVE MARINE LOBSTERS as Far as 1,800 Miles from the Ocean

The Most Comfortable Shoes You've Ever Worn or Your Money Back

Greatest Bible News in 341 Years

Free to Brides—$2 to Others

Weighs 86, Lifts 1,600

How to Save Money and Avoid Headaches in Transformer and Inductor Design

Which Plate Size Is Best for Electron Micrographs?

Answer These Questions and Work Out the Date of Your Own Death

 ## Action Point

Using one of your own products or services, write at least 15 different headlines on **Worksheet 4.** Then keep going for a total of 30! Use all of the methods you have learned so far. The more you generate, the better your opportunity for creating a headline that sells.

Worksheet 4

Headlines for Your Business Ads

As you create headlines for your products and services, use all of the ideas you have read about so far.

1. _____
2. _____
3. _____
4. _____
5. _____
6. _____
7. _____
8. _____
9. _____
10. _____
11. _____
12. _____
13. _____
14. _____
15. _____
16. _____
17. _____
18. _____
19. _____
20. _____
21. _____
22. _____
23. _____
24. _____
25. _____
26. _____
27. _____
28. _____
29. _____
30. _____

Chapter Five

27 Eye-Catching Ways to Use Illustrations and Photos

Read this information . . .	. . . complete this Action Point
27 Proven Guidelines	
A Secret about Graphics	
How to Test Your Illustration or Photo	Worksheet 5: Photos, Illustrations, and Graphics for Your Business Ads

Illustrations and photos serve the same function as headlines. They stop people who are sprinting through the newspaper or magazine. If they are done right, these graphics can help inform, persuade, and compel people. If they are done wrong, they can be a waste of money, a waste of space, and a waste of everyone's time.

27 Proven Guidelines

As Charles Austin Bates wrote in *Good Advertising* in 1896, "Take a lesson from the literary portion of the magazine. When an article is to be made interesting and prominent, it is illustrated. That's the thing to do with the ads." Here are 27 proven guidelines for enhancing your advertisements with illustrations, photos, or other graphics.

1. When targeting women, use women in your illustrations.

People identify with people who are like them. A common myth is that you should have an attractive male model to attract female buyers. But you are not selling sex; you are selling your small business or product. It is wiser to show a woman benefitting from your product if you are selling to women.

2. When targeting men, use men in your illustrations.

It is the same theory. If you run your ads in two different magazines, one read mostly by men, the other mostly by women, then you should adjust your ad to suit the audience. In the male-dominated magazine, use a male model in the ad. In the female-dominated magazine, use a female model in the ad. You will hear many people say you must use a woman in your ad to attract men. That is simply not the case. Placing a picture of a pretty lady in your ad *will* attract the eyes of most men, but they will be looking at the lady, *not* your ad! Remember, you are selling your product or service, not sex! Do not try to trick readers!

3. Show your product in action.

Products just sitting are boring. Show yours at work. If you have something that slices, dices, and cooks, show it working in your illustration. If you have someone who just bought a new suit from your store, show that person doing something in it. Action is much more revealing and appealing.

4. Show the end result.

If your toothpaste gives us brighter teeth, show a big smile of brighter teeth. If your product helps us lose weight, show us slim people. Show the end result—what people will get from using your product or service.

5. Tell a before-and-after story.

This is most often used with weight-loss products. But imagine a business that paints cars. The first illustration (before) can show the car dirty, aged, and rusting. The next illustration (after) shows the car freshly painted and looking like new. This technique is one of the most popular and effective methods you can use to illustrate your ad.

6. If appealing to the young or young at heart, use cartoons.

The funny papers are still one of the most popular sections of the newspaper. Use cartoons in your ad and people will be drawn to them. Years ago a test was done to see what part of the newspaper people wanted most. Few complained when the sports section was dropped one day. A few complained when the editorial pages were missing. But nearly *everyone* complained when the comics were missing from their newspaper!

7. Always run a caption under your illustrations.

People look at pictures and drawings and then look below them, searching for a one line description of what they just looked at.

Because this is common practice in all newspapers and magazines, people expect it. It is a good selling opportunity for you, too. Under the *after* photo for the painted car, a caption might read: "This car looks brand new because it was painted by Cooper Car Painters of Houston."

8. Babies attract nearly everyone.

Babies and young children work well in ads *if* you can justify their use. If you try to trick people into reading your ad, you will be considered conniving. You have to justify having the child in the picture. Showing a cute baby does not do much for an accounting firm. But if you can show the baby at the firm and say "We're the only firm that does taxes for the young and old alike," you might win some hearts.

9. Animals attract attention, too.

Dogs and cats work well in ads but, again, they have to somehow tie in to your advertisement to work well. Slapping a cute puppy on top of your ad will not get you any sales if the illustration does not have a logical reason for being there.

10. Use an interesting background.

You can liven up a boring item by taking a picture of it in an unusual or different background. Also, a fascinating background can give people a different feel for your product or service. For example, showing a picture of your new car wax in a bottle is not very interesting. But put the bottle on the hood of a shiny car parked in front of a mansion and you create interest, desire, and even romance.

11. Photos are more memorable than illustrations.

Photos are seen more, remembered more, and trusted more than illustrations. People feel pictures are actual representations of what was shot. However, illustrations may work better when trying to show details.

12. Be cautious with color.

While color does gain readers, it loses some credibility (people trust black and white as they are more accustomed to it in newspapers) and it costs a great deal more. Put one additional color in your ad and you will attract more readers, but ask yourself if this is worth the added expense. Try placing the extra color in your border, not in your photo.

13. Generate curiosity.

Get people involved. If you use a photo or illustration that snags people and makes them ask "What's happening here?" people will stop to read the ad and learn more.

14. People are interested in people.

Strive to have someone in your ad doing something. A crowd of people is not as interesting as one person *up to something.*

15. Show your face.

If you are running a small business where you are in contact with the public, run a picture of yourself. A speaker, for example, should show his or her face because he or she is the product being offered. People like to know who they are dealing with. Do not allow your ego to run away with you, however. Let any picture of yourself be one that helps *sell*, not just gratify your ego.

16. Put the headline below the illustration.

Because people read captions, your headline should be under your graphic. However, if your headline is run above the picture, also run a caption under the photo.

17. Use one dominant illustration.

One large, interesting picture can stop and involve readers. A couple of smaller ones can help demonstrate the product. But too many pictures confuse people, blur their eyes, and stop no one.

18. Attract the appropriate audience.

Use a photo or illustration that your target market will identify with. If you are offering a massage service, show someone getting their bad back cured. Getting attention for attention's sake is a waste of money. Target your buyers.

19. Be simple!

If you are selling shoes, show shoes. There is no need to be clever or creative. The people who are in the market for new shoes will look for shoe ads.

20. Reveal the benefit.

A picture of a plastic blanket covering a car effectively tells you what "Plastic Car Cover" does. If your photo reveals the benefit, your selling job is off to a nice start.

21. Consider a diagram, chart, or graph.

If your audience likes these, use them. Accountants may enjoy a spreadsheet while teenagers would not. Again, fit the illustration to your market.

22. Have the photo look at the reader.

Readers will follow the eyes of the people in your ads. If your ad has people looking off the page, readers may look off and away from your ad, too. Have photos lead into your ad.

23. Put the illustration at the top of your ad.

People tend to read from the top down. Catch them with the picture and they will look under it to read the ad.

24. Logos usually are not good illustrations.

Your logo (if you have one) is a brand but not a selling device. Do not run it as your illustration.

25. Show happiness.

Happy people in your ad says your product or service makes them happy. Do not show ugliness, show beauty. People buy end results. Illustrations of cavities do not sell; clean white smiles do.

26. Use the headline.

An ad does *not* need a photo or illustration to sell. If you cannot come up with an appropriate graphic, leave it alone. Strong headlines and body copy can make your ad a success. Your headline then becomes the graphic that pulls people in.

27. Show an incongruent graphic

If your headline says, "New Accounting Service Saves You Money" and your illustration shows something entirely unrelated, such as a man or woman sitting at home watching television and eating chips, people will stop and wonder what this is about. They'll *have* to read the ad to discover how the illustration fits with your headline. The object here is to intrigue and involve your readers so they are compelled to read your ad. the secret to making this tactic successful is to have a logical reason, explained in your ad's copy, for the illustration.

A Secret about Graphics

Your graphics—whether a photo or illustration—should gently *lead* the reader's eyes through your ad. That is why some graphic artists are smart enough to have a finger at the top of an ad pointing into it, which causes people to follow the finger and read the ad. That is why many photos have people either looking right at the reader, or down into the copy, again directing readers into the ad.

Your graphics should help make your sales message easier to grasp. They should help describe your sales message and also help make your message easier to receive.

How to Test Your Illustration or Photo

This is the same test you used to reveal the power of your headline. Ask yourself: Would this illustration or photo work equally well for my competitor's ads? If so, your graphic is not strong enough or unique enough for you. You want to stand out from the crowd.

 ## *Action Point*

Brainstorm different ways you can make your ad more captivating with photos, illustrations, and graphics. Use the list of 27 suggestions. On **Worksheet 5** make notes from your brainstorming about these ways to hook customers into reading your ads.

Worksheet 5

Photos, Illustrations, and Graphics for Your Business Ads

_____
_____
_____
_____
_____
_____
_____
_____
_____
_____
_____
_____
_____
_____
_____
_____
_____
_____
_____
_____
_____
_____
_____
_____
_____
_____
_____
_____

Chapter Six

How to Write Ad Copy That Makes People Buy!

Read this information . . .	. . . complete this Action Point
How to Create Hypnotic Copy	
How to Make Your Copy *Sexy*!	
Magic Words to Use	
More Tips on Writing Power Ads	
Ways to Generate Powerful Copy	
How to Turn Negatives into Positives	
Beware of Humor!	
How to Turbocharge Your Writing	
A Million Dollar Tip	
Three Ways to Test Your Ad Copy	Worksheet 6: Ad Copy for Your Product or Service Ad Copy Checklist Worksheet 7: Your Final, Polished Ad Copy
Hiring a Copywriter	
How to Read Copy from a Pro	Worksheet 8: Finding the Right Copywriter for Your Business Ads

$\mathbf{Y}$our headline and illustration hook the readers you want, but the words in your ad are what reels them in and makes them buy. "It is in body copy that your selling gets done—or it won't get done," wrote Clyde Bedell, another advertising genius from long ago. Writing *copy* (the words in an ad) to make an ad sell is an art. Many of the best copywriters in the world charge several thousand dollars to write the copy for *one* ad. Since most people with a small business cannot afford those fees, your other choice is to write the ad yourself.

How are you going to do it? How are you going to persuade people to your way of thinking? How are you going to talk people into coming to your small business and spending their hard-earned money?

This is probably the most challenging assignment there is when it comes to creating ads that hypnotize readers. The whole subject of persuasion is absolutely riveting. I am fascinated by what it takes to move people, to motivate people, to get them to act. As you and I both know, the pen is powerful. Writing can cause—or stop—wars. Writing can make—or break—sales campaigns.

How to Create Hypnotic Copy

What does it take to create hypnotic writing that persuades people to *your* way of thinking? That is the subject of this section. Here are the issues you need to keep in mind when creating writing that sways people.

Know What You Want

Before you do anything you must know what you want to accomplish. What is your goal? What is your objective? When people read your advertisement what do you want them to do? What action do you want your readers to take? What do you want your ad to accomplish?

Use Emotional Appeal

Back in the 1960s, Roy Garn wrote a thought-provoking book called *The Magic Power of Emotional Appeal*. Try to hunt down a copy. You will learn a lot about how to write ads in a way that captures people and makes them listen.

Garn's premise is that everyone—including you and me—is preoccupied. You have things on your mind. You are worried about money, work, your children, a new relationship, the future. Whatever. Or maybe you are thinking about sex, or a new movie you want to see, or a health problem. There is something on your mind right now, even as you read these words, that tugs at your attention. (Right?)

Our challenge as small business advertisers is to break people out of their preoccupation so they can hear what we have to say. If you do not shake your readers, they will stay preoccupied, and your writing will (so to speak) go in one ear and out the other—if it gets into an ear at all!

How do you break your reader's preoccupation? A quote, a story, a statistic, a headline, a name—all of these can help awaken people so they will take in your message. But the hook has to be relevant. For example, you can print the word "FIRE!" in big, bold letters at the top of your ad and you might get attention. But unless fire has something to do with your product or service, it is irrelevant to your potential readers. Be sure your hook logically fits with your small business.

Another approach is to meet your readers right where they are preoccupied. For example, if you are contacting writers, one concern (or preoccupation) of writers is the need to be published. So speak to that need. Tell those writers you can help them get published and you will connect with their emotional preoccupation. You have to ask yourself, "What does my reader care about?" and "What is on my reader's mind?" The people you are writing to probably have a common concern, problem, or complaint. Your ad should address that issue in a way that captures their attention.

Emotions move people. New evidence shows we make our decisions based on emotion and then rationalize them with logic. Appeal to your readers' main concerns and you will tap into their emotions with genuine appeal. And when you successfully do that, your copywriting becomes hypnotic!

Give Them What They Want

What do your readers want? No doubt they want real solutions to real problems. They do not want features, they want benefits. What is the difference? A feature is saying the new car has air bags; a benefit is saying the new car has air bags because air bags *save lives*. A *feature* states a fact. A *benefit* states why the fact is important to your reader.

Your readers want what most of us want: happiness, an easier life, security, entertainment. Can you give it to them? Can you help them achieve their dreams? Think of what your readers will get, not of what you want them to buy. You might want to sell your guitar repair service, but what people want are their guitars like new again. You might be selling a maid service, but what people buy are clean houses. There is a major difference.

Ask Questions That Lead to the Answer You Want

"If there were a way for you to write easily and powerfully, would you want it?" Obviously, if you are targeting the right group of people, there is only one way to answer the question—YES.

"If I could get you a new car at a monthly price you can afford and with all the options you want, would you be interested in seeing it?" YES, again.

And "If I could give you a marketing strategy that is guaranteed to increase your profits, would you be interested?" Of course!

Another, even safer approach is to ask questions that pull readers into your ad. In other words, rather than asking, "If I could solve your accounting problems, would you hire me?" you can ask a more involving question, such as: "What's the best way to solve your accounting problems?"

Use Word Pictures

Studies prove that we think in pictures. Describe your views, or your product, in vivid detail. Tell people what they will see, feel, hear, and taste when they use your new blender (or whatever). Paint a living portrait that people can see as they read your words. Have them *role play* in their mind what life would be like after doing business with you.

One secret to doing this is to tell your reader exactly what happens when they use your product. Make them *feel* what it is like. For example:

> When you turn on your computer, *Thoughtline* comes up, greets you by name, and then begins to ask questions about your project. You type in your answers and then *Thoughtline* asks you another question based on what you entered. Imagine how it feels to talk to your computer—and it actually talks back!

Get the picture?

Remind Them of the Problem—and Your Solution

Before you end your ad, remind your readers that they have a problem. Use that emotional appeal we mentioned earlier. Say, "If you're tired of receiving rejection slips, order my book today and put an end to your frustration."

Murray Raphel, coauthor of *The Great Brain Robbery* and *The Do-It-Yourself Direct Mail Handbook*, says fear is a great motivator: "Fear of loss is far more powerful than promise of gain." I do not encourage you to frighten people into seeing things your way, but I do suggest you gently remind your readers that they have a problem—and you have a solution.

If you are offering dental work, gently remind people that if they do not come to you, their teeth problems may become so bad that the cost and pain will paralyze them later. Be gentle with fear. If you are heavy-handed, you will scare customers off. Sell the end result, but gently remind them of what happens if they do not buy from you.

Be Sold on What You Are Selling

This may be the most important point. It is listed last because people tend to remember what they read last. You cannot sell what you do not believe in. This is a fundamental law in persuasion. How can you sell a car you would not drive yourself or a book you have not read or a software program you do not use? You cannot!

Enthusiasm sells people. And you cannot persuade anyone of anything unless you are first convinced. Emotional appeal and all the other tips will fall in line if you are sold on what you are saying. Do not try to write anything if you do not honestly believe in what you are writing about.

Follow the above guidelines, think about your readers' emotional concerns, and talk to them in a way they cannot ignore. If you do so, you will create copywriting that is both persuasive *and* hypnotic!

How to Make Your Copy *Sexy!*

How do you give your writing sex appeal? It is easier than you think. I will give you a clue: Which do you like to read: a novel by William Faulkner or your favorite mail-order catalog? The key to creating *sexy* writing is *format*.

William Faulkner was a literary genius who created classic novels. But his writings often had pages (pages!) of solid type with endless run-on sentences. You might have to search an entire chapter to find a period. Yes, Faulkner is considered a legend. No, most readers today do not want to see solid blocks of type. It is not very attractive. And it doesn't sell.

Here are four ways to make your writing more inviting:

- Use bullets
- Use quotes
- Use itsy-bitsy paragraphs
- Use boxes
- Use handwritten notes

Bullets

A bullet is a dot or star or asterisk. My list of four ways to create sexy writing was done with bullets. You can use bullets anywhere, anytime, and they will always work. They are a way to list ideas or key points. Bullets set off information on a page so it is easy to see, easy to read, and easy to grasp. They help break up text so readers feel they aren't "really" reading a whole page.

Quotes

Readers love quotes. Put something in quotation marks and it will get read before the text all around it. Why? Because people are interested in people. They want to know what was said, not what you want to say. As Horace said, "The musician who always plays on the same string is laughed at."

Little Paragraphs

Break up your ad copy paragraphs into one or two lines each. Stagger their length so they do not become predictable. Which would you read first—a letter single-spaced with no paragraph breaks, or a letter single-spaced with a two-line first paragraph, a three-line second one, a one-line third one, and so on?

Look at the following ad letters and tell me which is easier to read (they are the same letter)—which has more *sex appeal*. Is it **Exhibit 6.1** or **Exhibit 6.2?**

Exhibit 6.1. Ad letter

January 3, 1994

Dear Joe,

I am writing to personally invite you to my free workshop on how to achieve financial security. Anyone who wants to increase their estate by $500,000 to $1,000,000—with no added expense—will want to attend this event. Here's why: Recently I helped a dentist who had all of his savings in a 401K plan. As with most people, he had no idea that later his money will be ambushed by Uncle Sam. When he died, he would have left his family IN THE HOLE! Now he's secure. But that's not unusual. An older couple had their money tied up in CD's. I showed them how there is a better way to make money and now they will get $1,130,000—almost DOUBLE their profit! How is this possible? The secret is making smarter use of your money. What I do is reveal how to strategically place your money so you can become wealthy—quickly, easily, and safely. I call it Financial Engineering. And that's what I will explain in my two part workshop on January 18 and 25, Tuesday evenings from 7–9:30 pm, at 4265 San Felipe (7th floor). I will show slides and talk about these strategies. Then Leonard Roth, a local attorney, will talk about estate planning. There will also be time for your questions and answers. This event is free. I want you to come to this workshop as my personal guest, at no charge, and with no obligation, so you can see how I can help you reach your financial dreams. Even if you choose not to work with me after the event, you still will have gained some priceless insights about how to become wealthy today. My secretary will call you in a few days to be sure you received this letter, and to answer any questions you may have.

Sincerely,

Frances Corso
Financial Consultant

PS—Because of my schedule, I will not be giving this seminar again for some time. I urge you to mark your calendar and plan to attend. Let's make 1994 your year of wealth! To reserve your seat, just call my secretary right now at 621-1660.

Exhibit 6.2. Ad letter

January 3, 1994

Dear Joe,

I am writing to personally invite you to my free workshop on how to achieve financial security. Anyone who wants to increase their estate by $500,000 to $1,000,000—with no added expense—will want to attend this event. Here's why:

Recently I helped a dentist who had all of his savings in a 401K plan. As with most people, he had no idea that later his money will be ambushed by Uncle Sam. When he died, he would have left his family IN THE HOLE! Now he's secure.

But that's not unusual.

An older couple had their money tied up in CDs. I showed them how there is a better way to make money and now they will get $1,130,000—almost DOUBLE their profit!

How is this possible? The secret is making smarter use of your money. What I do is reveal how to strategically place your money so you can become wealthy—quickly, easily, and safely. I call it Financial Engineering.

And that's what I will explain in my two part workshop on January 18 and 25, Tuesday evenings from 7–9:30 pm, at 4265 San Felipe (7th floor). I will show slides and talk about these strategies. Then Leonard Roth, a local attorney, will talk about estate planning. There will also be time for your questions and answers.

This event is free. I want you to come to this workshop as my personal guest, at no charge, and with no obligation, so you can see how I can help you reach your financial dreams. Even if you choose not to work with me after the event, you still will have gained some priceless insights about how to become wealthy today.

My secretary will call you in a few days to be sure you received this letter, and to answer any questions you may have.

Sincerely,

Frances Corso
Financial Consultant

PS—Because of my schedule, I will not be giving this seminar again for some time. I urge you to mark your calendar and plan to attend. Let's make 1994 your year of wealth! To reserve your seat, just call my secretary right now at 621-1660.

Boxes

> People read what you put in boxes. Use boxes to highlight key points.

Handwritten Notes

You can add visual sizzle to your copy by including a few hand-written notes. For example, this comment probably leaped off the page and out of the book:

Look here!

Magic Words to Use

There are certain words which push positive emotional buttons in people. As much as you can, weave these words into your copy. According to Christopher Ryan, in *The Master Marketer*, those words are:

Announcing	Astonishing	Exciting	Exclusive
Fantastic	Fascinating	First	Free
Guaranteed	Incredible	Initial	Improved
Limited Offer	Love	Powerful	Phenomenal
Revealing	Revolutionary	Special	Successful
Super	Time-Sensitive	Unique	Urgent
Wonderful			You

To this list I would add these words:

Breakthrough	Introducing	New	How to

It is important to remember that if you just throw these words into your copy, you may appear to be adding fluff or puffery to your ad. You must always be specific and concrete to be believable. Saying your small business is "fantastic" is meaningless unless you describe what is fantastic about it. Saying you give "phenomenal" service persuades no one unless you describe how your service is phenomenal. Use the magic selling words in conjunction with the facts about your business. The combination will be explosive.

More Tips on Writing Power Ads

Be Specific

Details create credibility. Your shoe store may sell every size and brand of shoe on earth, but no one will believe you unless you spell it out. If you say "All Sizes Available," many readers will wonder if you have their size. Instead write, "Sizes 9 to 13 available." Specifics have power. That is why Ivory soap is "99 44/100% pure!"

Forest Wallace Cato, a famous promoter of celebrities, put it this way:

> Never write *animal* if you can write *dog*. And never use *dog* when you can use *Collie*. And never use *Collie* when you can say *old blind Collie with a missing left front leg*. Be as specific as you can.

Be Clear

Flowery writing or heady prose have no place in small business advertising. Say what you have to say as clearly as possible. If your customers or clients were standing in front of you, how would you talk to them? Write your ad as if conversing with one reader, and use the language that reader is most comfortable with. Leave no room for doubt. Imagine all the questions a reader may have, and answer them. If something is left out of the ad, the reader will not bother to call you and ask for clarity.

Be Enthusiastic

Whenever I am hired to write an ad or sales letter, I find out what is special or unique about the product or service. Then I describe it with "electricity." For example, a software program to help you think through projects can be called "New Software" or "Eye-Opening Breakthrough Software That Feels Alive!" If you are genuinely excited about your business, let that enthusiasm come through your writing. Excitement sells!

Be Complete

Say it all. Do not be afraid to write a lot of copy. You do not want to be wordy, but you do not want to cut off the ad too soon. People *do* read long ads just as they read long books. The only sin is a BORING ad. If your prospects are genuinely interested in your offer—and your writing is interesting—they will read every word.

Deliver a complete selling pitch in your ad. Without all the details, people will find a reason not to buy from you. If you wanted to send a telegram to invite a friend to lunch, you would not need very many words. Your copy would be short. But if you wanted to invite a stranger to lunch, and you wanted this stranger to bring along a check for $295 to buy your latest gizmo, you would need *a lot* of words to convince this stranger to show up. Your ad is very much the same. If you do not answer all the questions, no one will respond.

Be Helpful

Make your writing easy to read: Use short sentences, short words, short paragraphs. Make your copy visually attractive: Use ragged right margins, bullets, underlined words. Make it easy to buy: Give all the ordering information. Give people what they want, not what you want to sell them. Help them make their lives easier and they will do business with you.

The bottom line is this: What is in it for the buyer? Think of the people who may buy from your small business. How can you help them? Focus on that in your ad.

Ways to Generate Powerful Copy

Tell a Dramatic Story

Describe a story about someone who used your product or service and was better for it afterwards. For this to work, jump right into the story with action. Leap into the drama. A good story-ad begins with something happening. This action sweeps people up and moves them along. If you tell the story well, they will read every word with excitement.

Conflicts are engaging. Write your ad with as much excitement and color as you can, showing a problem and a resolution. Someone with a knee problem might be fascinated to hear the dramatic story of how one of your customers was helped by your medical service. Focus on *one* person. A flood that destroys 3,000 homes is not as moving as the story of one family that survived the ordeal.

Ask and Answer Questions

One of the best ways to communicate ideas is to ask questions that buyers might have, and answer them. If you are clear about what your prospects need to know, this interview format can be very persuasive and easy to write.

Talk about What People Get

Focus on the end results of using your service. People do not care about specifications or boring details—they want to know what they will get. Write your copy while always thinking, "You will get this from my product or service" and "You will get this" and "You will see this happen" and so forth. Paint a vivid picture of what people will get from using your small business. Be interesting.

Follow Your Headline

The headline you create will steer you in a particular direction. Follow it. If your headline is a question, your ad copy should answer it. If your headline is a statement, your copy should support it. If your headline says "Here Are the Two Best Ways to Handle Your Taxes," your ad copy should of course describe those two best ways.

Give the *News*

Tell your readers something they don't know. Give information. I call this method "Reveal the Business Nobody Knows." When people need chiropractors, all they know is their backs hurt and they want relief. If you run an ad that answers "What You Need to Know Before You Choose a Chiropractor," you will get business. Why? Because you are giving people information they can use—and it just happens to be information that establishes you as the expert and the person to call.

How to Turn Negatives into Positives

What do you do if you have something perceived by the public as negative? Master copywriters know how to handle this situation. Whether your price is considered too high, your location too far away, or your product or service limited in scope, there are ways to change customers' perceptions.

One way is by comparing your negative in a way that makes it understandable. If your refrigerator repair service costs $60 an hour, you might say: "Our service is guaranteed to repair your fridge. Since a new refrigerator costs $600, spending *one-tenth* of that to get your old one as good as new is a real bargain!"

Another way to alter people's perceptions is to explain your negative with a logical positive reason. If your small business is located twenty minutes from the city, you might say: "We're located right outside of the city—away from busy streets and dangerous areas so you can relax and enjoy safe shopping in our store."

If you are a consultant working out of your home you do not have to be defensive about not having an office. Your ad can say: "I am one of the few consultants left who actually serve you by making house calls. You don't have to leave your home or office— *I'll come to you!*"

If your negative is a problem to people, *listen to them* and change what you are doing to please them. When Henry Ford started his small business, he told customers, "You can have any color you want—as long as it's black." Customer demand forced Ford into changing his negative into a very real positive!

Beware of Humor!

Some of the most famous advertising campaigns that were based on humor *failed*. People may laugh, chuckle, or just grin when they read your ad, but they typically *do not buy* as a result of humor. Humor is the most dangerous form of advertising you can try. As noted in Chapter Four on headlines, not everyone has a sense of humor, not everyone agrees on what is funny, and few people buy from clowns.

Again, are you selling good feelings or your product or service?

How to Turbocharge Your Writing

The following seven steps present an easy method that can help you with any kind of writing task.

1. State your intention.

   Do you want calls, orders, faxes, visits, or appointments? What do you want your ad to achieve? Write this down for your own use. This intention will not end up in your ad copy.

2. Do your homework.

   Make notes about your selling points, benefits, audience interests, etc. Be thoroughly familiar with everything about your offer.

3. Write the first draft *fast*.

   Sit down and write—as fast as humanly possible—the first draft for your ad. Write everything that comes to mind. Do not edit. Do not think about it. Do not stop. Write and continue writing—even if you think it is trash—until you have completed an entire draft. Imagine you are writing a single letter to a particular individual to sell them on your small business.

4. Take a short break.

   Go get a cup of coffee. Stretch. Breathe. Relax.

5. Write another draft.

   Put the first draft aside and write another one, from scratch, and as fast as you can. Again, no editing, stopping, or concern. Just do it!

6. Take a longer break.

   Put your drafts aside for a few days (if possible). Your unconscious mind will work on the ad copy while you keep yourself occupied doing other things.

7. Edit the ad.

   Make your ad perfect. Look at your drafts. Combine parts, cross out sections, add missing paragraphs. Show the copy to others (particularly anyone in your target audience). Get feedback. Edit some more. Ask yourself: Does this ad do what I intended for it? Many of the best copywriters throw out the first ten paragraphs of whatever they write!

A Million Dollar Tip

The best way to learn how to write persuasive copy is to read successful copy. Find ads that have worked and study them. Try to figure out what makes them work. It is the best copywriting education you can get—and it is free!

But do not study ads you *think* are successful. Study ads that have been *proven* to work. The three following examples of small business ads will help get you started in that direction.

A Successful Flyer

The first example, "You Can Make a Fistful of Dollars With a Few Little Sketches," is a successful flyer used to sell a book. Notice the strong headline, clear benefits, guarantee, and order form. This ad is designed to get *results*—and it does. Up to 25 percent of the people who see this ad order the book!

Exhibit 6.3. A Successful Flyer

You Can Make a Fistful of Dollars With a Few Little Sketches
(Using Little or No Talent)

How would you like to turn a favorite hobby or pastime into an exciting moneymaking venture?

Well, now you can! If you've ever thought about earning prestige as an artist and making money in the process, you owe it to yourself to read: *BIG BUCKS FROM LITTLE SKETCHES: Proven Ways to Earn Money with Portraits and Caricatures Using Little or No Talent.*

In this exciting work by Roscoe Barnes III, you will learn what it really takes to survive as an artist. Whether you're a veteran artist or just starting out, *BIG BUCKS FROM LITTLE SKETCHES* will help you to PROMOTE YOUR TALENT and TURN DOODLES INTO DOLLARS.

Increase Your Popularity . . . Boost Your Self-Esteem!

The fact is, SKETCHING PEOPLE IS A SUREFIRE WAY TO BOOST YOUR INCOME and INCREASE YOUR POPULARITY. You could also BOOST YOUR SELF-ESTEEM. There are opportunities in every locality, and Roscoe uncovers those opportunities in your own hometown.

Perhaps you've heard: "Ain't no money in art. The field is over-crowded. Too competitive!"

Don't believe it! Art is alive and well. Just look around you. It's everywhere! One kind, however, sells faster than others. That kind is SKETCHING PEOPLE . . . in the form of portraits or caricatures. They continue to be HOT-SELLERS.

A Ready Market Awaits You . . . Now!

A few artists know the value of sketching people. They make BIG BUCKS as a result. And you can, too!

Continued

Here's why:

* People of all ages enjoy seeing themselves drawn or painted, and will pay big bucks to have it done. "If you can draw people well," said Jack Hamm, "you become a wanted individual in both commercial and fine art."

* Unlike the typical Fine Artist, you don't have to wait for a gallery or exhibit before making a fast buck. And you don't need an agent.

* People like to laugh and they like to have their pictures drawn, says Stan Barker in *The Artist Magazine*. "If you have a flair for cartooning and a feel for people . . . caricatures can be a market that is rewarding for both body and soul."

* Sketching is the most INEXPENSIVE art medium. Equipment can be obtained at any reputable art store.

* Sketching can be done almost ANYWHERE and at ANYTIME.

With these factors in your favor (and there are others) YOU CANNOT LOSE! Find out today by ordering your copy of *BIG BUCKS FROM LITTLE SKETCHES*.

Hit the Ground Running!

In eight fact-filled chapters, Roscoe uses practical instructions and workable ideas to get you started in a hurry.

Among other things, you will learn:

* How to DISCOVER and DEVELOP YOUR TALENT for sketching people.

* How to DEVELOP a LEGITIMATE SUBSTITUTE for the talent you may think you need.

* How to SET UP YOUR STUDIO and arrange your equipment.

* How to PREPARE A WINNING PORTFOLIO . . . one that'll enhance your image and improve your credibility.

* How to FIND THE CUSTOMERS who are willing and ready to buy your sketches.

* How to PROMOTE YOUR WORK on special holidays and other occasions.

* How to use your sketches to IMPRESS your school, city officials, friends, relatives and employer.

* How to EFFECTIVELY REACH your customers on a day-to-day basis.

* How to SET PRICES that customers will pay.

* How to DEAL WITH BURN-OUT.
  Plus much, much more!

Included in this extraordinary work is a useful list of WINNING TIPS that will help ensure your success. You will also get pages of helpful resources on PROMOTION/PUBLICITY, BUSINESS, TALENT, and ART INSTRUCTIONS.

Learn from An Accomplished Artist, Writer, and Teacher

As you open the pages of this step-by-step guide, you will be absolutely amazed at the hundreds of ideas you could apply—in one day! Also, you will find comfort and assurance because of the author's background:

Roscoe Barnes is a professional artist with 20 years of experience. He's an award-winning writer and popular speaker. Drawing on his wealth of experience, he will guide you every step of the way!

Everything You Need . . . Simple and Easy to Follow

BIG BUCKS FROM LITTLE SKETCHES is THE ONLY MANUAL OF ITS KIND. It is THE MOST EXHAUSTIVE work you will find on SKETCHING PEOPLE FOR PROFIT. Even more, it's packed with simple, no-nonsense, and easy to follow instructions.

Satisfaction Guaranteed

Why not order your copy of *BIG BUCKS FROM LITTLE SKETCHES* . . . TODAY? The cost is only $13.95. Follow the instructions for 30 days. If you are not completely satisfied, return the manual and your cost will be refunded.

To order, simply fill out and return the attached coupon below. Include payment. And your future as a *money-making* artist will be off to an exciting start!

_____ YES! I want to make a fistful of dollars with a few little sketches! Please rush me a copy of *BIG BUCKS FROM LITTLE SKETCHES* for $13.95 (plus $2.00 for postage & handling). I must be able to make money sketching people in 30 days or my entire payment is refunded.

I have enclosed $_____ as the total for my order.

Name _____

Address _____

City _____ State _____ Zip _____

Mail to: Roscoe Barnes III
           P.O. Box 4382
           Gettysburg, PA 17325

A Successful Sales Letter

The next example, from Experience in Software, Inc., is a sales letter offering a new software program. Note the *news–benefit* oriented headline. It snags the reader and pulls that reader into the strong narrative copy. This letter gets about a 9 percent response—while the typical sales letter gets about a 2 percent response!

Exhibit 6.4. A Successful Sales Letter

EXPERIENCE
IN SOFTWARE, INC.
From the Creators of "Idea Generator" & "Art of Negotiating"

• •

Announcing—Breakthrough New PC Program—Reveals
How To Plan Direct Routes To Success
—For Any Project—In Only 30 Minutes—
With Results Guaranteed!

• •

<u>Exclusive</u> Introductory Offer For Preferred Customers Only

Dear Friend,

About a month ago a writer friend of mine asked what I had been working on. I pulled out "Project KickStart". I told him it was simple to use, it took little PC memory, and you could use it to create a strategy for any new project. He looked skeptical.

"Any project?" he asked. I nodded. "Let me try it then."

I watched him load the program, type PKS and view the screen. Though he wasn't a computer whiz, he just followed the menu and was typing answers in seconds. I noticed he seemed to like the interactive quality of the program. Project KickStart asked questions, he answered them, and he kept moving.

Just when I was about to get a cup of coffee, he stopped typing and looked right at me. I thought something was wrong.

"I'm done," he said.

I couldn't believe it! I asked him what he had worked on and he said, "I have to write a book proposal, so I tried the program out on that. It gave me some sharp ideas I probably would have overlooked or never thought of without it." Then he added, "Not bad, Roy."

Continued

How I Discovered Project KickStart

About two years ago I noticed many of my customers were using "Idea Generator", our popular creativity tool, for projects. Right then I began to write the program that became Project KickStart.

I wanted to capitalize on the strength of "Idea Generator" while making Project KickStart a stand-alone tool. I wanted Project KickStart to help you create an action plan that you could use—for any project, no matter what it was—and preferably within minutes.

And I wanted Project Kickstart to be something you could print out, or view on your screen, or even down-load into all the various project management programs you might already use.

I have nothing against these scheduling programs, of course. They are marvelous for tracking results, but they are lousy for helping you create the front-end thinking you need before you ever begin a project. And that's why I wanted Project KickStart to work by itself, and _then_ easily and quickly hook up with these project management programs.

More Evidence Project KickStart Works

Michael Chambers of Teck 5 Corp. said, "I wish I had this last week when I was doing the initial set-up in Time Line. KickStart would have saved me hours of work. With Project KickStart I can lay-out a project in 20 minutes that took me 2 hours in Time Line."

Consultant Joseph C. Fusco, quoted in _PC Week_, said, "Project KickStart helps you at the general strategy level—it gives you a task-generating technique that helps you see the forest. Project management software deals with the individual trees."

The Possibilities Are Astonishing

What projects are you working on—or thinking about?

Project KickStart can save the day and make you the hero. When I was a lawyer with the Federal government, I used to pray for someone to walk into a meeting with a strategy already worked out. Now that can happen! Now you can focus on _results!_ Now you can get things _done right!_

Are you launching a new product? Planning a career move? Or, even moving your office? Project KickStart will help you test feasibility, map out tasks, prepare for obstacles, and even delegate jobs. And it all happens surprisingly fast and easy.

Iron-Clad 60-Day Money-Back Guarantee

You'll get results—I _personally_ guarantee it.

Try Project KickStart for 60 days. If you don't create eye-opening new strategies, if you don't save time and money, if you don't get a workable plan within 30 minutes, then I'll refund your money. No questions asked.

Continued

Please note that Project KickStart will sell for $195.95 (or more) very soon. But you can get the program right now for only $79.95. This special introductory offer is <u>strictly limited</u> to 30 days! You must call today—right now—to grab this bargain!

Call **1-800-678-7008** right now—and begin to plan for success!

Yours for achievement,

Roy A. Nierenberg
President

PS — Remember, "Project KickStart" will help you create strategies for <u>any</u> project you can think of. You'll get results within 30 minutes—guaranteed! You can have the program right now for only $79.95. Use it once and you'll save much more than the cost of the program. After that, any time you use the program, it's FREE! But you must act today. The price leaps up after 30 days! Call right now!

A Successful Card Deck Ad

This final example of a proven sales ad, for a "Personalized Marketing Strategy," is a card deck advertisement used to sell a marketing service. Note how the magic word "Free!" makes this headline irresistible. The copy establishes the writer as an expert. What is missing is a deadline to encourage people to act now. Some readers waited one entire *year* before responding! Still, this advertisement pulled a 5 percent response and generated several thousand dollars in profit.

Exhibit 6.5. A Successful Card Deck Ad

Get A FREE "PERSONALIZED MARKETING STRATEGY!"
From The Wizard Of Words Who Has Earned Millions For Others . . .
Now Let Joe Vitale Make Big Money For You—*GUARANTEED!*

Amazing? Not really. I do it by writing irresistible $$$-making copy that persuades and compels people to buy NOW!

Experience pays: I've written books, feature articles, sales letters, ads and more—all for businesses like yours. All have gotten remarkable RESULTS! One client is now criss-crossing the US giving talks on his new book. Another had to open a franchise to handle all the new customers! Her business soared! Talk about making money!

Now it's your turn: I can't predict the results you'll get but I can certainly guarantee your TOTAL satisfaction! (After all, I wrote a book on giving excellent service.)

ADDED BONUS: When you become my client, you also get my marketing know-how. I'm known as a marketing samurai with the "knack" for success. Frankly, my ideas can help your business SKY-ROCKET! Ready? Then hurry. My client list is nearly full!

Just return this card and I'll do the rest. The information is free. There's no obligation. And your complete satisfaction is fully guaranteed. What could be better?

PS – You can speak to me PERSONALLY by calling (713) 999-1110 right now!

Three Ways to Test Your Ad Copy

Here are three proven ways to run a preliminary test on your copy:

1. Let a twelve-year-old read it. Since the average consumer has a reading level skill of a teenager, this method can be an eye-opener. Let a reasonably intelligent twelve-year-old read your copy. If your reader does not understand it, do the copy over.

2. Let a few potential customers and clients read the copy. If they say, "This is well written," you have failed. What you want them to say is, "Can I buy this from you?" You want them to become excited and ask to do business with you. If they read the ad and are not interested in your product or service, go back to the drawing board. Do the ad again.

---

3. Read the ad and ask yourself if this can be used for your competitors. If it can, do it over. You want your uniqueness to stand out. If anyone in a business similar to yours can run the ad, the ad is not finished. Make it yours alone.

 ## *Action Point*

You are now ready to write your ad copy. Everything in the book up to this point has prepared you for this! Complete **Worksheet 6** first as a draft. Use the worksheet as a guide to stimulate your thinking, but do not be locked into this structure. Allow yourself the freedom to be creative but always remember your job is to *sell!* Then, using the techniques covered in this chapter, polish it into your final copy. That is not the last step, though! After you have completed that final copy there will be a checklist and an opportunity to re-write your final corrected copy on **Worksheet 7.**

Worksheet 6

Ad Copy for Your Product or Service

1. Write your headline.

   _____

   _____

2. In your first paragraph, grab the readers and shake them. Continue
   to earn their attention by expanding on the headline. Use quotes,
   testimonials, stories, statistics, a shocking statement, benefits, a
   guarantee, or whatever you feel will pull readers into your ad.
   Remember, *think of your readers!*

   _____

   _____

   _____

   _____

   _____

   _____

   _____

3. Tell the readers why the ad is important. Make them see and feel
   what you are talking about. Dramatize your product or service. Make
   it come alive in their minds. Pretend you are talking to a friend and
   paint a vivid picture of your business.

   _____

   _____

   _____

   _____

   _____

   _____

   _____

4. Now prove your claims. Give testimonials from satisfied clients, or state your guarantee, or describe what is unique about your small business in a believable way. Give details. Be specific. Be sure to tell the readers what is in it for them!

_____
_____
_____
_____
_____
_____

5. Now move in for the close. Tell the readers why they need to act now. Is there a deadline? Will they get a free gift for calling today? Remind them of what happens if they do not buy today. Make the readers want to buy your product or service NOW. If you do not prod them into responding right now, they will probably *never* respond.

_____
_____
_____
_____
_____
_____
_____

6. Ask for the order! Tell your readers what to do: Call, write, fax, visit, fill out a coupon. Be sure to give all the details on how to reach you. Describe exactly what the readers are to do to benefit from your product or service. Do not leave it up to them and do not give too many choices. Tell them exactly what to do.

_____
_____
_____
_____
_____

Action Point

After completing your polished version of your ad copy, go over this checklist. Then use **Worksheet 7** to write your final copy.

Ad Copy Checklist

After you have written your first draft, and polished it, use the following to check your ad's potency.

1. Does your opening pull readers into the ad with fast, compelling, strong reader interest? Does the opening begin with a BANG?
2. Does the copy move along at a swift, easy-to-read clip, generating desire all the way? Is it boring?
3. Is the copy written in the conversational style of the person who is going to read it? Have you spoken on the same wave length as your readers?
4. Is the copy visually attractive and inviting, using short sentences, short words, short paragraphs, bullets, subheads, and other visual aids?
5. Does the copy overcome objections and answer all questions? Is the ad a complete selling argument?
6. Does the copy include proof and create believability with testimonials, specific details, and a guarantee? Can your prospects read this and remain skeptical?
7. Does the copy end with a powerful call to action—a request to fill out a form, call, or visit your business? Do you tell readers what to do?
8. Is the copy written from the viewpoint of what the readers will get? Do readers know how their lives will be improved?
9. Is it clear what you are selling? Is there one central offer?
10. Does the copy reveal what is new, unique, or different about your small business? Can your competitors also use this copy?
11. Is there a deadline or some other logical reason for a reader to act *now?* Can your prospects read this and put the ad aside to respond later?
12. Are there plenty of reasons to buy? Since people want to buy, have you convinced them why they should?
13. Does your copy follow and complete what your headline begins?
14. Have you reminded your readers of what happens if they do not buy?
15. Have you tightened the copy so you say what you have to say in the fewest words possible? Have you let others edit the copy for you?
16. Is this the best you can do? (Are you being honest?)

Worksheet 7

Your Final, Polished Ad Copy

_____
_____
_____
_____
_____
_____
_____
_____
_____
_____
_____
_____
_____
_____
_____
_____
_____
_____
_____
_____
_____
_____
_____
_____
_____
_____
_____
_____
_____
_____
_____
_____
_____

Hiring a Copywriter

Since your expertise may not be writing, you may want to hire a copywriter. But how do you choose the right copywriter for you? What do you look for? Is the copywriter you have (if you have one) the best for your needs? If so, how do you know? If not, how do you select the perfect one for you and your small business?

How do you know what to ask for? These are guidelines that will help you make the best choice.

Mail-Order Experience

Mail order is ruthless. You spend money on mailing lists and postage and you either get results or not. There is no rationalizing that "the advertising was good for our image."

Your copywriter should have a proven track record of success selling items by mail. Far too many copywriters in ad agencies have NO experience in mail-order direct selling. They may have won awards for cleverness, but unless their ads produced results, they may not be right for you.

Psychology Experience

A good copywriter understands how people behave—and why they buy. You have to know how people think to know how to persuade them to buy from you. People have unique motivations. A smart copywriter knows them and uses them to advantage.

Skilled therapists can help clients change because they understand the client's unique "inner map" of the world. Your ideal copywriter should have practical experience in psychology, preferably in working directly with people in a counseling situation, to understand how those "inner maps" work. Since it may be very difficult to find a writer with this kind of background, look for someone who has demonstrated a skill at writing ads for different types or groups of people.

Though people have common basic motivators (greed, lust, power), the buttons you have to push to engage those emotions are different for different people. A good copywriter knows this—and knows how to use it to your advantage. An article in *Printers' Ink*—in 1895—stated, "Probably when we are a little more enlightened, the advertising writer, like the teacher, will study psychology."

Direct-Selling Experience

Many legendary copywriters started by selling products door-to-door. That is a priceless education. You quickly learn what it takes to get attention, hold it, deliver your message, and close the sale. Any copywriter without personal selling experience is not going to be as effective as one with it. A copywriter who has had to knock on doors or make cold calls or work in a small store selling direct to individuals is going to have firsthand experience of what it takes to motivate people to buy.

Proven Writing Skills

Writing ability is important. Most copywriters know how to write, but not how to write in a skillful and persuasive fashion. Most people think they can write; most people are wrong. Persuasive writing is an art and a trade that takes decades to learn. Knowing how to weave words in a strategic manner takes a writer with tremendous skill and experience. You want someone with proven skill in nonfiction writing, and preferably writing that has had to sell.

Willingness to Learn

It is not essential that your copywriter be an expert in your field. If your copywriter is willing to learn about you and your product, it can be a successful relationship. Look at the copywriter's samples. Are they written for a variety of products? Also, a copywriter does not have to have experience in writing business-to-business copy, because executives and other so-called sophisticated types are also consumers. They, too, respond to the tried and true methods of persuasion.

How to Read Copy from a Pro

You hired a copywriter to create an ad for you, so the number one thing you do not want to do is rewrite those words! Trust the expert. Do not change words or sentences because you think they are grammatically incorrect. Copy often violates rules of English in order to make a sale. If you have questions about the copy, ask your copywriter. If you do not understand the strategy or intent, ask for clarification.

Do not let others edit the copy, either. Some of the worst copy ever written was done by "committee." If your ad has to be approved by your staff and your relatives, your ad's strength will probably die in the process. David Ogilvy said the greatest ads ever written were usually done by two people: an employer and a copywriter. You are the employer who hired the copywriter. Tell the copywriter what you want to sell and achieve and let that professional go to work.

 ## *Action Point*

If you have decided to use a professional copywriter, you must know how to make the right choice for your business. If you have already hired a copywriter, you should review your choice to ensure you are getting the best results. Use **Worksheet 8** when interviewing for a new copywriter or reviewing your current situation.

Worksheet 8

Finding the Right Copywriter for Your Business Ads

1. Does the copywriter have samples of completed work?

2. Has the copywriter written for a wide variety of products or services or at least for a business similar to yours?

3. Were the ads successful? If so, how do you know?

4. Does the copywriter have mail-order experience?

5. Has the copywriter worked selling to people in person?

6. Do you have good rapport with this copywriter?

7. Can you trust this copywriter to do the best work for you?

Chapter Seven

How to Use Testimonials, Guarantees, and Coupons

Read this information . . .	. . . complete this Action Point
The Power of a Quote	
How to Get Testimonials	
Get Permission!	
Overwhelm Your Buyers	
Million Dollar Advice for Using Testimonials	Worksheet 9: Testimonials and Endorsements for Your Business
The Best Guarantee	
The Best News of All	
How to Create a Guarantee	
The Most Successful Guarantees	Worksheet 10: Creating the Guarantee
Everyone Cuts Them Out	
How to Create a Coupon	
One Drawback to Coupons and One Warning	Worksheet 11: Creating Your Coupon or Gift Certificate

In this chapter we will look at three techniques you can use to make your ads succeed: testimonials, guarantees, and coupons. Many small businesses do not take advantage of these ad components, but they are simple and effective tools. Testimonials will have your customers doing your selling. Guarantees will build confidence in your business. And coupons will *make* people respond to your ads.

The Power of a Quote

What is the best way to convince people that your dental practice, beauty salon, or accounting firm is the one to hire? How do you persuade strangers to do business with you? What is one of the most powerful ways to create credibility in your ads? The answer to all three questions is the same: Testimonials.

Testimonials are so potent that you can run an ad with *nothing* but testimonials (and your phone number) and you will get more responses than most other advertisers! A *testimonial* (a quote testifying to the excellence of your business from a satisfied customer or client) is a third-party endorsement. It is considered objective. It is also considered the truth. You can write and run all the ads you want. If you are astute and follow the guidelines you have learned so far, your ad will get results. But you will get even more results when you use testimonials in your ads.

With endorsements from satisfied customers, you are not just saying you are a good business, you are *proving* it. I can write a sentence saying, "I write compelling copy." Does it do much for you? Probably not. But if the president of a large company says, "Joe Vitale writes compelling copy," you will tend to believe it. It is the difference between bragging and hearing an expert opinion.

How to Get Testimonials

Acquiring testimonials is easy. All you do is *ask for them!* I have a mental program that kicks on whenever I hear a compliment about my work. I automatically say "Thank you," and then add:

"Will you put that in writing for me?" Ninety percent of the time I get the testimonial I ask for.

Ask your current satisfied clients to write a testimonial for you. If they seem reluctant, you can make the request less threatening by asking it this way: "Will you jot down a few lines about my service?" Many people do not like to write. But asking them to *jot down* a few thoughts sounds (and is) easy.

If they still do not want to write the testimonial, offer to do it for them. Then write down what you think they want to say and— this is important—show it to them for their approval.

You can also solicit testimonials by simply asking your customers and clients how they are doing. If they say they are doing well because of your small business, that is your cue to ask for a testimonial!

You can rest assured that people like to give testimonials. They are flattered you asked, and they know they will see their names in print when you use their quote. Your more astute clients will realize this is an advertising opportunity for *them*. In fact, you should point that out to them. Whenever you run your ads with their names in it, they get *free* publicity! (And for that reason you should never be reluctant to give a testimonial to anyone who asks it of *you*.)

Get Permission!

Always ask permission to use a testimonial! If you receive a letter in the mail from a satisfied client who raves about your service, do not assume you can print that letter. The letter is in your hands, but the words are still the property of the person who sent it. Your customer's words are covered by "common law" copyright. You must get the writer's permission before you print anything they write, or else you can fall into legal problems. Bob Bly, author of *The Copywriter's Handbook*, suggests you send a "standard permission letter" to your customers.

The opening of this letter greets your customer with thanks for the recent testimonial. Next, either reprint the testimonial or attach a copy of it. The next line says you would like to reprint the testimonial in your ads. Then write: "If this is okay with you, would you please sign the bottom of this letter and send it back." Enclose two copies of the letter, one for the customer to sign and return to you, the other for the customer's own records. Bly also suggests you include a SASE (self-addressed stamped envelope) to make responding easy for your customer.

Tips for Power Testimonials

1. Tell the truth.

   It is illegal and immoral to fabricate a testimonial.

2. Reveal the source.

   Give the entire name, not initials. People think quotes with initials are fake. It is also wise to include the person's city and state.

3. Show status.

   If the testimonial or endorsement is from an accountant or the President of the United States, say so. This adds credibility.

4. Be specific.

   "The massage was great" is a weak testimonial because it is vague. "The massage loosened up my back and now, for the first time in weeks, I can walk without pain!" is powerful because it is specific.

5. Be natural.

   Testimonials do not have to be written well. The more they sound like natural, everyday conversation, the more believable they will come across.

6. Show clear benefits.

   "Tom Jones' legal services saved me money" reveals a benefit. But notice what happens when you combine this with a *specific* benefit: "Tom Jones' legal services saved me $3,498 with only one phone call!" The latter makes the reader reach for the phone.

7. Put them in quotes.

   Always put quotation marks around your testimonials. That tells people this is an endorsement, and it is also visually attractive on the page or in your ad.

Overwhelm Your Buyers

Today people are phenomenally skeptical of advertising. You cannot blame them. They have been tricked by fake contests, false claims, and misleading offers. Consequently, people are guarded. Your ad may make them *want* to buy, but this lingering skepticism will often prevent them from doing so.

How do you overcome this mindset? One of the best ways to handle their fear is to *overwhelm them* with testimonials. Get all the endorsements you can. Pile them on. There is no such thing as too many. Lawyers call it having a "preponderance of truth." If you have a sheet of paper with nothing but testimonials on it—front and back—people will automatically assume your service is tops.

People will not even need to read the page, either. Just *seeing* a page (or ad) crammed with solid testimonials is very persuasive. This is why many books have several pages of testimonials in the front of them. A friend of mine bought Harvey Mackay's book, *Swim with the Sharks Without Being Eaten Alive*, because of the pages of endorsements in it. "Any book that loved must be great," my friend said. And he bought *six copies* of it—*before* he ever read the book!

Million Dollar Advice for Using Testimonials

1. Avoid using celebrity endorsements.

Research shows quotes from celebrities (movie stars, famous athletes, etc.) fail for two reasons: People remember the star and not your product or service, and people assume the celebrity was paid to give the testimonial.

2. Expert opinions sell.

If you are running a bakery and a famous chef says your cakes are the best she's ever tasted, *that* is a testimonial with power. People tend to believe the opinion of acknowledged experts. Do not be afraid to write or call experts. Their addresses are usually available through the library (by looking in *Who's Who*, for example) and most are flattered that you ask for their opinions. Michael Jordan's endorsement for "Air Jordan" shoes obviously helped sell that product.

3. Obtain testimonials with rewards.

John Caples, in *How to Make Your Advertising Make Money*, said he often ran small ads offering cash prizes for the best testimonial letters in order to generate a file of usable endorsements. He suggests running an ad that contains an entry blank coupon, such as:

> Finish this sentence in 25 words or less: I like (name of your product or service) because _____
> _____
> _____
> _____
> _____ .

4. Use a good testimonial as your ad's headline.

A short quote that reveals benefits and arouses curiosity can make a terrific headline. If your dental practice was praised by a bank president, consider using that statement as the headline on your next ad. Keep in mind that the headline still has to capture the attention of the appropriate audience and that all of the suggestions for making a good headline still apply. The difference is that your headline is being *spoken* by someone, and that gives it color and life.

5. Keep them short.

You can tighten long-winded testimonials by leaving out words and substituting ellipsis (. . .). "His method of teaching the guitar is easy, yet effective, and he gives cookies after class" can be tightened to read "His method . . . is easy, yet effective . . .". Remember that you must have permission from the person to do this editing.

6. A lot of testimonials can make an ad.

You can even run an ad with nothing but testimonials and your phone number in it. Place a riveting headline at the top of your ad. Then fill the space below with descriptive testimonials. End with a call to action (your phone number, or a coupon, etc.). If your testimonials tell the story, your work is done! That is the ad!

7. One long compelling testimonial can be an ad.

If you are lucky enough to receive a long, glowing, fact-filled letter about your small business, you may have an ad already written for you. Is the letter complete? Does it tell your story? Does it answer your buyers' questions? If so, consider running the entire letter—with permission, of course—as your next ad.

8. Add their photos.

You make your testimonials even more persuasive by including a photo of the person who gave the endorsement. This is rarely used by anyone but is remarkably effective in creating trust. While some customers may remain suspicious of testimonials, adding a photo tends to create confidence.

Testimonials That Work

"As a direct result of your marketing advice I received 15 radio interviews, and over 80 newspapers and magazines requested review copies of my book."
—Bill Ferguson, author, *How to Heal a Painful Relationship*

"Sue's accounting saved me from paying $10,000 in extra taxes last year. I completely endorse her work."
—Mel Therman, CEO, Landwater Photos

"I hired your cleaning service because a friend told me you did top work and I wanted my place PERFECT. You came in and cleaned, washed, waxed, and more. I am very impressed and will also hire you."
—Susan Favor, Detroit Homemaker

"Your donuts are what get me going in the morning 'cause they have that home-baked grandma's kitchen taste that makes me feel happy and ready to take on the world."

—Detective James Martinez, Dallas

 ## *Action Point*

Start collecting testimonials for your own small business. You can begin with **Worksheet 9** right now by listing twenty people (clients or customers) you can contact. If they cannot write the quote, or jot one down, offer to write it for them and show it to them for their approval.

Keep in mind that this is also an opportunity to find out what is *wrong* with your business. If people have a few negative comments, hear them and use that as feedback in perfecting what you do.

Worksheet 9

Testimonials and Endorsements for Your Business

People I will contact for testimonials:

1. _____
2. _____
3. _____
4. _____
5. _____
6. _____
7. _____
8. _____
9. _____
10. _____
11. _____
12. _____
13. _____
14. _____
15. _____
16. _____
17. _____
18. _____
19. _____
20. _____

The Best Guarantee

Who would you rather hire:

- a printer who guarantees his or her work or one who does not?
- an interior designer who guarantees your satisfaction or one who does not?
- an insurance agent who guarantees coverage or one who does not?

I am astonished at the number of small businesses that are hesitant to guarantee their services. If you are doing good work, why *not* guarantee what you do? If you have a reason to fear people will not be happy with your service, take a clear look at what you are doing and improve the weak areas so people do not have any reason to complain.

You *need* a guarantee today. Since you are not the only person in your line of business, you have to somehow outflank your competition. Having a strong guarantee is one way to do that. Without a guarantee, people will remain skeptical of you. Even with a guarantee, they will have reservations. But a guarantee weakens the risk. When you have a guarantee, new clients find it easier to try you out. They feel safe. They know that if they are not happy with you, the guarantee will set things right again. The guarantee is their security blanket. But without a guarantee, they may never test you. It simply will not be worth the risk.

The best way to create a guarantee is to make it risk free for your customers and clients. Put all the risk on *you*. You can see how powerful this can be by imagining yourself as a customer. If you want to buy a new VCR and one model is guaranteed and the competing model is not, which will you buy?

Clearly the company that offers the guarantee is taking a risk. But just as clearly, they will get your money. Guarantee *your* product or service and you will get the business.

The Best News of All

I advised a small publisher to guarantee the directory he was printing and selling. He refused, saying "It's a good book."

"If it's a good book, why not guarantee it?" I asked.

He shrugged and said, "No one ever asks for their money back."

"That's exactly why you should guarantee your book!" I said. And that's exactly why *you* should guarantee what you do.

The reality is that less than two percent of your customers and clients will ever act on a guarantee. Most people are simply too lazy or unaggressive to complain or ask for their money back. (They *will* complain to their family and friends, however, and that is why you should always be striving to deliver flawless service. You do not want anyone out there bad-mouthing your business.)

What this means to you is that you will get more business by having a guarantee than not having it, and you will rarely, if ever, be asked to honor the guarantee. (Of course, if you are asked to honor it, then you legally must do it.)

How to Create a Guarantee

1. Tell your customers and clients exactly what they will experience from using your product and service.

2. Tell your customers you guarantee their satisfaction. Prove it by offering their money back if they are not happy.

3. Strengthen your guarantee by putting an extended time limit on it. "Guaranteed for ten days" is a lot weaker than "Guaranteed for 30 days" and that is a lot weaker than "Guaranteed for 365 days—one entire year." The longer the guarantee, the more business you will get because people will feel safe. A "lifetime guarantee" is the most powerful of all.

4. Strengthen your guarantee even more by offering a "double your money back guarantee." This is riskier for you, but remember, very few people will ever ask you to enforce your guarantee.

5. You can make your guarantee almost irresistible by offering "triple your money back" if not satisfied.

6. Put your guarantee in an official-looking box in your ad so people can easily see it. A strong guarantee is a selling point. Flaunt it. Make it stand out.

7. If your guarantee is a real eye-opener and a complete selling message, consider running it as your headline.

   "NEW! 10 Minute Makeovers—Guaranteed!"

8. Sign your guarantee. People like to deal with people, not a business. If you stand behind your guarantee, put your signature to it.

9. Name your guarantee. Call it "The *your name* Guarantee."

10. Make your guarantee a certificate your customer can have. It is very reassuring to hold an official-looking guarantee!

The Most Successful Guarantees

A small business music catalog in Woodstock, New York, uses this guarantee:

> **The Homespun Guarantee:** All Homespun audio and video lessons are unconditionally guaranteed against technical defects. If you ever have a problem with any tape, regardless of when you bought it, return it to us and we'll gladly replace it with another copy of the same lesson.

Sears, Roebuck and Company—which began as a VERY small business—has successfully used this powerful guarantee for nearly 100 years:

> **The Sears Guarantee:** *Your satisfaction is guaranteed or your money back.* We guarantee that every article in this catalog is accurately described and illustrated. If, for any

reason whatever, you are not satisfied with any article purchased from us, we want you to return it at our expense. We will exchange it for exactly what you want, or will return your money, including any transportation charges you paid.

A famous mail-order ad to sell Sanaton pipes to smokers had a guarantee so effective it put the small business two months behind in filling orders:

If not satisfied after your 10-day trial, break the pipe, send me the pieces—no charge.

The guarantee from L.L. Bean is also powerful:

All of our products are guaranteed to give 100 percent satisfaction in every way. Return anything purchased from us at any time if it proves otherwise. We will replace it, refund your purchase price or credit your credit card, as you wish. We do not want you to have anything from L.L. Bean that is not completely satisfactory.

Raphel Publishing in Atlantic City has sold thousands of books and tapes and has *never* had a return. Their long-term guarantee is a winner:

If, for any reason, you are unhappy, dissatisfied or fail to come up with money-making ideas from any book, tape or video you purchase from Raphel Publishing, send it back to us for a complete and immediate refund. This guarantee is valid for a full year after you purchase your product, no questions asked.

Action Point

Now it's time to write a guarantee for your own small business. One place to begin is to look at your competitors. Do they offer guarantees? (Look in the phone book's yellow pages or your local papers to see their ads.) Can you top them? How can you make your guarantee stronger? Use **Worksheet 10** to develop your own guarantee that will top your competition and sell your product.

Worksheet 10

Creating the Guarantee Your Customer Needs

1. Write your competitor's guarantee (if they have one) here:

   _____
   _____
   _____

2. Write your own guarantee (or make one up) here:

   _____
   _____
   _____

3. Now strengthen your guarantee by offering a longer time limit (30 days, 60 days, 6 months, a year, for life, etc.):

   _____
   _____

4. Make the guarantee even more powerful by offering as much as you can. Can you make it a double- or even triple-your-money back if not satisfied?

   _____
   _____

5. Be sure your guarantee spells out the benefits of your small business. If it does not say what people will get from using your service, add this to your guarantee. Example: "After taking this new Power Negotiations seminar, you'll be able to close more deals than ever before with less stress, guaranteed or your money back." Does your guarantee express benefits? If not, add it now. What will people *get* from using your service or product?

   _____
   _____
   _____

6. How can you make your guarantee even stronger? Brainstorm some ideas here. Let your mind be free and write down what you create:

_____

_____

_____

7. Now rewrite your entire guarantee to include the best of everything you have come up with so far:

_____

_____

_____

_____

Everyone Cuts Them Out

Notice all the ads for small businesses in your local newspaper. And notice how many times all you see are their names, logos, phone numbers, and photos of themselves. Those ads do not cause anyone to respond because they do not *ask* anyone to respond. They are there to create an image. The problem is, in today's fierce economic society, your image will probably never be noticed unless you have got millions of extra dollars handy to try (and I mean *try*) to influence the public.

A wiser strategy is to create an ad that causes people to act *now*. One of the best ways to do that is to include a coupon in all your ads. Just having a coupon in your ad tells people "here is an offer" and "here is something for me to do." Since all of your ads should do their best to involve the reader, a coupon is a sound way to pull a person into your advertisement. An ad with a coupon will get as much as six times more responses than the very same ad without a coupon! Put coupons in your ads!

One of my clients is an interior designer. I was helping her devise an ad and suggested she put a coupon inside her ad. She looked stunned and said, "Coupons are for lower-level consumers!"

"They are?" I asked, knowing that coupons have been effective for *everyone* since 1910 and the days of advertising pioneer Claude Hopkins.

"Businesses that use coupons aren't doing very well," my friend announced.

"Look, Debbie," I began. "Coupons have been proven to work over and over again. People look for them, expect them, cut them out, collect them, act on them, and look for more. Every business that uses them pulls in more business. That's why coupons are used so much. And that's why over 300 *billion* coupons were printed last year alone!"

"But I'm going after an elite clientele," she said.

"Then call your coupon a gift certificate. One of the reasons rich people are wealthy is because they know how to manage and save their money. They like coupons, too!"

My client didn't realize that people—no matter what their income level—respond to some of the same motivators, such as health, fear, envy, power, sex and, yes, even greed. Coupons encourage people to buy now because it gives them a logical reason to act now—an incentive to buy the product or service they have been wanting.

How to Create a Coupon

1. Restate the offer.

What are you selling? Whatever it is should be said again in your coupon. If you are offering something free, or a special low price on your service or product, SAY SO. People can read the coupon and get your message.

2. Put a time limit on it.

If you want people to act now, put a deadline in your ad. Make the time limit reasonable and logical, but do not leave it out. Without a deadline, people may put the coupon aside "for later," and then forget it forever.

3. Make it look like a coupon.

You have seen coupons. They are usually small, rectangular, and have a heavy dashed line around them as the border. Make your coupon look like a coupon. One of my clients (against my advice) once printed a "coupon" on a full 8 1/2" × 11" sheet of paper. Very few customers cashed it in because it did not *look* like a coupon!

4. Place it at the bottom-right corner of your ad.

That is where people expect to see the coupon.

5. Consider the other side.

If you run your ad in a newspaper or magazine, consider buying the space on the back of the page. If there is an important article on the flip side of the page, people may not cut out your ad. But if you buy the space on the back of your ad—if only the space where the coupon is—people will not lose anything from their news. This may be expensive, but worth it in the long run. When you buy the ad space, consider saying "See ad on other side" to encourage people to look.

6. Leave room for writing.

If you want readers to fill out their name and address, etc., on your coupon, leave plenty of room! My first publisher sent out a coupon to people announcing my book and the spaces he left for people to write in were so small no human could possibly do it! And if anyone could squeeze their information into that space, no other human could read it. Give plenty of space for fill-in-the-blank coupons.

7. Tell them what to do.

Do not leave it up to your readers. If you want them to call, tell them. If you want them to write, tell them. Add a line that says "Clip and mail" or "Cut this out" along the dotted edge of your coupon. Giving people a direct command increases your replies.

8. Give the information they need.

Remember to give your phone number if you want them to call; to give your address if you want them to write. Leave out any important information and people will not be able to respond because they will not know how.

9. Restate your guarantee.

Since you now have a powerful guarantee, restate it in the coupon. Many of your readers may look at your coupon before they read your whole ad, so be sure your coupon carries your heavy artillery— your guarantee.

10. Run it as an ad.

If your coupon is a complete sales pitch, consider running it as an ad. It will not cost you as much as a larger ad and yet people will still spot it and read it.

11. Give it out.

If your coupon is complete, duplicate it and offer it as is, just as many other small businesses do. One of the most successful pizza delivery services in the world—which also began as a small business—has been giving out coupons every year, nonstop, because it *always* brings in more business.

12. "Key" your coupons.

You can trace the effectiveness of your coupons by "keying" them with your own secret code. All you have to do is write something on one set of coupons that you do not have on any other coupons. For example, if I want to know how many people write to me as a direct result of reading this book. all I have to do is list my address and add something like "Dept. A12" to it. Every letter that I receive with that on it is a dead giveaway that they heard of me from this book.

If you are running your ads in several publications, you will want to know which ad is getting the most attention. In one ad write "Dept A12," in another ad write "Dept B13." If you get more "Dept A12" coupons back, then you know that publication is bringing you a lot of business. You can then decide to run more or bigger ads in that source.

13. Make it easy to cut out.

Try to place the ad on the bottom of a page so people only have to make two cuts, or two rips, to get the ad out. If it looks like work to tear out the ad, they will not do it.

14. Use an illustration.

If possible, print a small graphic of your product or service, or you, in your coupon. Since a coupon is very much like a "mini ad," having a graphic helps tell people what you are selling.

15. Use a headline.

Again, since the coupon is a small ad, a coupon restating the offer or benefit helps drive your point home. Example: "*Free* Tax Review!"

16. Make it unusual.

Sometimes an unusually shaped coupon can get more attention. Consider a coupon in the shape of a circle or a triangle. It must still look like a coupon, of course, but the shape of it can be changed to draw in more eyes.

17. Call it something else.

Since some people in business do not seem to like coupons, you can call your coupon a "gift certificate."

One Drawback to Coupons and One Warning

There is one negative point about coupons that you should be aware of. People get used to them. And expect them. And will learn not to buy from you without them.

As with the pizza makers I mentioned earlier, if you give out lots of coupons, people will become trained to only buy when they have a coupon. The way to remedy this is to either keep running coupons and change them with better offers or lower prices, or run them only three or four times a year.

The Warning

The interior designer mentioned at the start of this chapter is right to be concerned about coupons *if* the coupons are to be used to offer a discount on your professional service.

A coupon suggests a savings or a free item of some sort. That is natural. But if you use a coupon to give a discount on your professional service, you may lose some credibility. Imagine a brain surgeon who says "Brain Surgeries—10% Off With This Coupon!" Would you go to her? Hardly. But if she offered a coupon that entitled you to a free booklet about brain surgery (and assuming you were in the market for one), you might clip that coupon out.

Offer coupons for products, but be careful offering them for services. One way around this dilemma is to call your coupon a "gift certificate." Any professional can offer gift certificates and reap the same benefits that come with having coupons. Same theory, different name.

 ## *Action Point*

You can create (or improve) your own coupons by walking through the seventeen steps I just described. Complete **Worksheet 11** and you will be ready to put your completed coupon or gift certificate right into your polished ad.

Worksheet 11

Creating Your Coupon or Gift Certificate

Design your coupon from the steps in the chapter. Then answer these worksheet questions. If you need to change your coupon, do that now!

1. What is your offer? What are you selling to people? _____

2. What is your deadline?_____

3. Does it look like a coupon? _____

4. Did you place it at the bottom right of your ad? _____

5. What will be on the other side of your ad in the newspaper or magazine? Can you purchase that space, too?_____

6. Have you left enough room so people can write? _____

7. Have you told people exactly what you want them to do?_____

8. Did you give your phone number and address and other essential information? _____

9. Can you restate your guarantee in the coupon? _____

10. Can you run the coupon as a separate ad? _____

11. Can you duplicate the coupon and give it away?_____

12. Have you "keyed" your coupons so you can trace results?_____

13. Is the coupon easy to cut or tear out of your ad? _____

14. Can you use an illustration in your coupon?_____

15. Do you have a strong headline? _____

Chapter Eight

How to Create Explosive Direct Mail

Read this information . . .	. . . complete this Action Point
How to Write a Sales Letter	
Bruce Barton's Secret Formula	
The Magic of a Good List	
The Most Important List	
Your Offer	Worksheet 12: Creating a Direct Mail Campaign

Small business owners often tell me they are afraid to use direct mail. They are right to be cautious but wrong to dismiss this opportunity. "You'll only get a 2 percent response if you're lucky," one dentist told me. "That's a 98 percent waste of money." I quoted him the line by John Stevenson of Private Marketing: "We got rich being 2 percent right, so we didn't worry about being 98 percent wrong."

The fact is, direct mail advertising accounts for 29.2 percent of *all* advertising expenses (even beating television's 26.6 percent). When you consider that you are lucky to get one half of one percent response to your print ads, direct mail looks like the promised land.

And do not think people hate mail. According to a 1988 U.S. Postal Service study, 72 percent of postal customers really like to receive and read direct mail ads. People are not as overwhelmed by their mail as you may think, either. The average person receives only three pieces of mail advertising *a week!*

You can acquire more business than ever before if you follow the proper guidelines on creating effective direct mail. The three most important elements are your *offer*, your *list*, and your *sales letter*. Of the three, your mailing list is the most important. But all three have to be thought out or your mailing will probably bomb. Perfect these three items and you and your small business can profit beyond belief.

Direct mail requires its own book. What I will describe here is *one* way to get results. We begin by looking at your sales letter.

How to Write a Sales Letter

Here are eight steps to creating a sales letter that will get you the results you want. Some of these points will duplicate what you read earlier in the chapter on how to write copy. They are so important that they are worth repeating.

Make Your Letter Personal

Think back to the last time you went to your mailbox. You pulled out a handful of mail. You thumbed through it all. What did you open immediately? Of course you opened your *personal* mail. If the envelope had your name handwritten or typed on it, you knew it was for you and not a sales letter for anyone at your address.

Any time an envelope has teaser copy on it ("Special Offer for You Alone!") or a mailing label on it (a dead giveaway) or a bulk rate stamp on it (another giveaway), you know the letter is probably junk mail. And you probably toss it in the trash. Most people do. To influence people you have to make your letter look personal. How do you do that?

Start with the envelope.

- Do not put any teaser copy on the envelope. Let the envelope look like something that has a real letter from a real person in it. While many famous copywriters can develop teasers that get attention, I am suggesting you try this safer approach. If you insist on using a headline on your envelope, some good ones include "Immediate Reply Requested," "Confidential Information," "Please Read at Once," "Personal," and almost any handwritten message.

- Put a hand-affixed first-class stamp on the envelope. Bulk rate and even meters make the envelope look impersonal, cheap, and cold. (I once received a colorful, impressive, and official-looking envelope with the words "Overnight Express Mail" on it. The bulk rate stamp told me the envelope was a lie. It was really a sales piece.) While many studies say it does not matter what type of stamp you use, I disagree. First class creates a better first impression and is delivered faster. And first class *gets delivered*, while third class sometimes does not.

- Address the envelope by hand or with the address typed or printed right on the envelope. I know labels are simpler and faster. But do not think of yourself, think of your client. If you want to make your client buy, find ways to make the envelope look personal. Using a font that looks like handwriting is an example.

- Address the envelope to someone in particular. Do not send your letter to "occupant" or "personnel manager" or "the boss." Send it to a real person and use a real name. (How personal and powerful is "Dear buyer" anyway?)

Make the letter personal—or at least personal looking.

- Use the type style you normally use in your business. I am assuming that your font is something very easy to read. The impression you want to give is that this letter is a personal communication from you to your customer.
- Use your letterhead. Personal letters are done on your stationery. If you do not have a photograph of yourself on your letterhead, get one. People want to know who they are dealing with.
- As with your envelope, address the letter to an individual. You can do this with a mail-merge program and your computer. If that is not possible for you, a weak second choice is to address the letter to the particular group of people you are after. If you are writing to computer programmers, you can begin the letter with "Dear computer programmer." It is obviously not as effective as "Dear Sarah Jones" but it will work.

Do not deceive people. Some people send out a sales piece in a card that looks like a wedding invitation. When the client receives it, the first response is delight at being invited somewhere. But the second response is resentment at being tricked. You do not want to increase people's resistance to your offer. If you are sending out a letter, let it look like a letter. If you are sending out an invitation, let it be an invitation to a real event (a special sale, a grand opening, etc.).

Use Emotional Appeal

People are busy. Whether they are busy with work or busy day-dreaming, they are always preoccupied. Your letter is an intrusion into their world. They are not expecting your letter and are not really excited about reading it (not yet, anyway). How do you make these people wake up and read—*and act on*—your words?

You have to create emotional appeal. You have to tell the reader what you have that will make that reader's life better. The only way to do this is to appeal to your reader's emotions—and you have to do it right away. The best way to accomplish this is to use a powerful headline and opening sentence. You need something short and catchy that speaks directly to your customers' interests.

Answer the questions: "Who cares? So what? What's in it for me?"

Every person who gets your letter will ask themselves these questions and you have to be able to answer them. What *is* in it for your reader? Too many writers think of themselves, not their customers. I say get out of your ego and into the reader's ego! What does your customer want?

Turn their desire into a headline.

If your particular clients are people who want their computers repaired, a headline might be "Have Your Computer Running Again at 486 Speed!" Rather than offering your repair service, offer what your customers want, which is the finished product or end result.

Let your headline pull the reader in.

Put the headline on the left side of the page, at the top, under your letterhead and above your opening. Your readers will see the headline and, if you made a headline that speaks to their interests, it will pull them right into your letter. If your business practice does not allow headlines, then the first sentence of your letter should be the headline.

Tickle their interest.

Be sure that your letter's opening line also tickles your reader's interest. A few powerful ways to begin a letter are:

- With a question

  Would you like to have your own book published for added credibility, more publicity, and more money?

- With a quote

  "A book is the only immortality." Rufus Choate

- With a statistic

  There are over 1,000 books published every week. But very few are by popular speakers like yourself.

Speak It

Articulate, lively people often turn into wordy bores when they write. Far too many writers still think they have to use big words when expressing themselves on paper. What a mistake!

People like to read short sentences, short paragraphs, and short words. The average reading ability (of those Americans who can even read at all) is on the ninth-grade level. Complicated writing and long letters do not make sense, do not get action and usually do not even get read. The way around this is to write the way you speak. That is not to say it is okay for you to say anything you want, however you want to say it. Rather, this is a suggestion for you to write in a colloquial way. Write as naturally and as easily as you speak. Use contractions, use "I" and "you," and be yourself.

Do not write to impress, write to express.

- Pretend your customer is standing in front of you. What would you say? How would you speak? Write *that*. (It is a good idea to record the actual talk, transcribe it, and then edit it.)

- Go through your letter and delete every word that you do not normally use—or hear used—in conversation. A rule of thumb is to be sure your letter can be understood by a twelve-year-old. And while you are at it, delete all the "I"s you can and insert "you"s—focus on the reader!

- Present your sales pitch as an explanation. Focus on what the customer gets, not on what you want to sell. Giving reasons for buying and stating benefits for buying sound much more persuasive.
- Paint a vivid picture of your customer's life after the purchase from you. What will be easier for the customer? Give an example of someone else who bought from you and is now very satisfied.

Here is a secret for making your letters almost impossible to avoid reading: Show dialogue. A conversation livens up *any* letter and makes it very inviting to read. You can often convey a complete sales message by simply writing a conversation between two people.

Give Proof

The number one reason people do not buy from you (or anyone else) is a lack of trust! You and I and everyone else have had the experience of reading a great letter, buying the product, and then being disappointed when the item did not live up to what the letter claimed. People have been burned too many times to trust anyone now. To handle this, offer a guarantee (you should *always* offer a guarantee) and offer proof.

Give testimonials in your letter. You need three to five quotes from *real* people. Saying "J.W. in Kansas City" liked your product is not believable. Saying "John Williams, President of Flight Control Operations, Kansas City" liked it, is persuasive. And if you can get a testimonial from someone the reader may already know and respect, all the better.

Ask for What You Want

It is amazing how many people do not ask for what they want. Just recently I read a powerful two-page letter from a Houston business-man that had me ready to cut off a leg to buy his product. But I did not buy. Why? Because he did not ask me to! He failed to ask for the order.

What do you want your readers to do? Tell them! It is most persuasive if you remind the readers of their problem, or of what they will get when they buy (or what will happen if they do not buy), and *then* ask for the order.

Use a Postscript

What is often read first, last, and remembered longest? The PS! Put your strongest selling point in the PS and your message will last longer. Copywriters spend hours, even days, writing powerful letters. They have plenty of time to put their message in the body of the letter. But they always use a PS! And for good reason. It is your opportunity to hit the reader—hard!—with the strongest reason for buying.

Make It Attractive

Visual impact accounts for 70 percent of your letter's effectiveness! A letter dense with type, with small margins, no paragraph breaks, and no bullets, does not get read. Make your letter attractive. Make it inviting.

Ideas for Making Letters Attractive

1. Use ragged right margins. Readers unconsciously use the right margin to guide their eyes as they read. Leave it ragged.

2. Use wide margins, but not too wide. One inch all around is fine.

3. Skip a space between paragraphs. Also, indent the first sentence of each paragraph and keep the paragraphs short.

4. Use bullets. You can list important points, or benefits, in an attention-grabbing way by using a star or a dash before each point.

---

5. To highlight a point, put it in a box.

6. Use dialogue. "Dialogue works!" exclaimed James Smith.

7. Add handwritten notes. A brief handwritten note brings a letter to life, even when you will reproduce that letter.

8. Use "connector" words such as "and" and "but" and "or."

9. Do not end a first page with a complete sentence. A broken line at the bottom encourages people to turn the page and keep reading.

Sharpen the Knife

Writing a letter that makes people do what you want takes skill. By following the above principles you will create a letter that people will read. But there is one more thing you have to do to complete the process: You have to edit your work to perfection.

How do you know if your letter will get the results you want? Make ten copies of your letter. Hand them to ten friends and associates. Ask for their feedback. You will get free editing (people love to mark up drafts). You will also find out if your letter pulls. If these ten people do not express any interest in your offer, rewrite your letter. Make your letter persuade.

Bruce Barton's Secret Formula

Bruce Barton, legendary advertising figure, wrote letters that got *staggering* results. He wrote fund-raising letters for Deerfield Academy that broke all records and helped raise enough money to secure that Academy's future. He wrote a letter for Berea College that brought in an amazing *100 percent response!*

When you consider that the average successful letter gets about a two percent response, Barton clearly leaped way past anyone else in his letter writing skills. But what was his secret? How in the world did he ever get such high responses from his letters when so many of us barely nudge up to the two percent response rate?

After studying Barton's letters, books, private memos, speeches, and advertising campaigns for my last book, I discovered Barton's "secret formula." I have used this method to write my own letters and I have been astonished at the results. In an essay he wrote back in 1925, Barton said that good advertising copy (and letters are advertisements) had to be three things:

- Brief: "About sixty years ago two men spoke at Gettysburg; one man spoke for two hours. I suppose there is not anyone who could quote a single word of that oration. The other man spoke about three hundred words, and that address has become a part of the school training of almost every child."

- Simple: "I think it might be said, no advertisement is great that has anything that can't be understood by a child of intelligence. Certainly all the great things in life are one-syllable things—child, home, fear, faith, love, God."

- Sincere: "I believe the public has a sixth sense for detecting insincerity, and we run a tremendous risk if we try to make other people believe in something we don't believe in. Somehow our sin will find us out."

Brevity

A short letter is not necessarily what Barton meant. I have read many of his letters and memos. Most of them were so brief they were blunt. But those were not *sales letters*. When Barton wanted to persuade you to donate money to a good cause or buy something he was selling, his letters were longer, sometimes several pages long. Barton knew you had to give people a complete explanation before they would buy. His letters were long enough to state his case— and not a word longer.

Simplicity

Barton's letters were always simple and easy to read. As with everything he wrote, he strove for clarity of communication. No big words, long sentences, or convoluted passages. He was clear and direct and conversational.

Sincerity

Barton was *always* sincere. He once dropped a million-dollar account because he did not support the client. That sincerity came through in everything he wrote. You could *feel* it in his letters.

Finally, Barton's letters were ". . . phrased in terms of the *other man's interest*." Barton said your letters had to go straight to the reader's selfish interest to be successful. He said the favorite song of every reader is "I Love Me." As Barton said in 1924, "The reader is interested first of all in himself. . . . Tie your appeal up to his own interests."

The next time you have to write a letter, consider Barton's formula. It helped him write letters that are still talked about today. Use it and see what the formula will do for *you!*

The Magic of a Good List

Where you send your letter is of crucial importance. You cannot send a letter about your new ice cream parlor to readers of *Weight Watchers* magazine. Those readers are not your potential buyers. To make your direct mail advertising effective, you have to match your business with those who will be interested in your business. You have to target your prospective buyers. You have to go after those people who have expressed an interest in your product or service.

To do this, start and keep your own list of customers. This is your gold mine! Call a mailing list broker for help. These brokers act as consultants who match your business with the right list. They do not charge a fee because they make a commission on the lists they rent to you.

Look in the back of your yellow pages under mailing lists and you will find a few local brokers to call. You can also call any of these nationally-known mailing list houses, each of which has their own brokers on staff. While you have them on the phone, ask them to send you their free catalog of mailing lists.

Database America, 1-800-223-7777
Edith Roman Associates, 1-800-223-2194
Hugo Dunhill Mailing Lists, 1-800-223-6454

Tell the broker what type of business you are in. It is their job to match you up with the appropriate list. They will make a few suggestions, and it is your job to check out the lists. Do not assume anything. Here are some questions to ask:

- How much is the list rental? You can expect to pay anywhere from $50 to $100 per 1,000 names, with a 3,000 name minimum order. This is to *rent* the list, which means you get to use the names once. It is illegal to use them more than once if all you did was rent them. (Of course, once someone has bought something from you, they go on your own list.)

- Is the list guaranteed? Since people tend to move and change address on a regular basis, how accurate is the list? Will the broker guarantee that the list is at least 95 percent deliverable?

- How old is the list? The newer the list, the better. Never get a list older than six months. Again, this will reflect whether the addresses are still good or not.

- How were the names on the list compiled? If the list is made up from names and addresses out of a phone book, it is a *compiled list* and is not what you want. It is always better to rent a list that is made up of people who bought something similar to what you are offering, and who bought it through the mail. This is called a *response list*.

- How big is the list? You may not care that the list has only 3,000 names. But if you are planning an ongoing direct-mail advertising blitz, you may be more interested in a list that has a total of many more names.
- Can you see a complete description of the list? A good broker will mail or fax you a complete description of the list you are interested in. That description should answer all of your questions.
- Is the list available as peel-and-stick labels or in some other form you can use?

Never immediately buy a list. Check it out thoroughly. Since this is one very important aspect of your mailing's success, completely investigate the list. You might even ask for a random sampling of the list. Though not done very often, some brokers can give you 100 names for you to test. The problem is, you usually cannot tell very much from such a small mailing. Most tests are done on a mailing to 5,000 names.

The Most Important List

Finally, keep in mind that the most priceless list of all is *your own list*. You should be getting the names and addresses of every person you have ever done business with and keeping this information on a database. This is your *hot list*. There is no one more likely to buy from you than the people who have already bought from you. Your goal should be to obtain as many names as possible for your own list, and then consistently contact these hot leads with new offers.

Most of your profit will come from the people on your own mailing list. In fact, it is often worth a loss on a direct mail campaign just to acquire new names for your own house list. The reason being that once these people are on your list, you will sooner or later sell to them and make a profit.

Your Offer

What are you selling?

Why should people buy from you?

What are you offering?

How is it better or different than your competition?

What is your USP—unique selling proposition?

Answers to these questions help reveal your offer. You need an offer of some sort to persuade people to contact you. One of the most common is to offer something free that is relevant to your business and your market. Another method is to offer a discount on your product or service. Here are three examples of offers:

- FREE skirt when you buy a blouse at our women's store
- 50% OFF on dinner when you bring a friend to our deli
- FREE booklet on how to tell when your car needs a tune-up

Though you always want to make a sale, keep in mind that what you also want is a new name—a hot new lead to add to your database. You may not even care if these people buy from you at this time. What you want them to do is raise their hand and say "I'm interested in what you have to offer." When that happens, you put their name on your house list.

And then you continuously send these people new sales letters, or even postcards, about new offers. Stay in contact and you will create a relationship with these people that will be profitable for you.

 Action Point

With the points covered in this chapter, direct mail should no longer be intimidating! Put together a direct mail campaign for your product or service. Use **Worksheet 12** to put your completed components all together.

Worksheet 12

Creating a Direct Mail Campaign

1. What is your offer? What are you selling? What is unique about your product or service? _____
   _____
   _____
   _____

2. Who is your target audience for this offer? Who would most be interested in your small business? _____
   _____
   _____
   _____

3. What mailing lists are available that fit your offer to your market? (Call a list broker or two and get their suggestions.)
   _____
   _____
   _____
   _____
   _____
   _____

4. Is the list guaranteed deliverable? _____

5. Is this a compiled or response list?_____

6. Write a letter to sell your offer to the people on this list. Keep in mind that your letter needs to be personal, friendly, attention getting, and offer a clear, sound benefit. In many ways, writing a sales letter is like writing a good ad. You should have a headline at the beginning and a call for action at the end. Remember Bruce Barton's tips and keep your letter simple, sincere, and brief.

7. Now *rewrite* your letter.

8. Can you personalize the letter or the envelope? If so, you will increase responses.

9. Can you mail first class? Though it costs more, you will also get more responses. If you have to go third class, use a stamp, not a meter, on the envelope.

10. Have you given people a way to respond? You will get more replies if you include a return-reply card or an order form.

Chapter Nine

How to Make Classified Ads Work for You

Read this information . . .	. . . complete this Action Point
One Example	
Classified Ads *Can* Work	
When to Use a Classified	
How to Write a Classified Ad	
Classified Ad Examples	Worksheet 13: Writing a Classified Ad That Will Have Results

From time to time small business people will ask me about classified ads. I tell them to avoid buying classified ad space to sell products. I tell them I think it is too often a waste of money. Say you want to advertise in the classifieds of *USA Today*. Though the paper had a seven year rocky rise to stability, it is now a popular and respected national daily. But is it a good place to advertise?

One Example

USA Today has about 6,000,000 readers. That is an estimate, of course. Magazines and newspapers tend to say their publications get passed around, and with that justification they multiply their subscriber base and tell us their estimated readers. Their actual subscribers are far less. We will say they have 1,000,000 readers. It still sounds pretty impressive.

But those million readers do not read the *entire* paper any more than you or I do. Some read the lottery numbers, others the sports pages, still others the entertainment section. Most of the time the only people who read the ads are the ones who *placed* the ads. But to be fair about this, we will assume that at least ten percent of the actual readers will get to look at the classifieds. That means we have about 100,000 possible customers. And that still sounds good.

Of that 100,000, how many do you think read all the classifieds? Better yet, how many do you think will read *your* particular section in the classifieds? It is hard to guess, but we will say ten percent will get to your ad section. That means 10,000 people will see your ad.

Of those, how many will actually respond? This is the kicker. It is tough to get people to respond to a tiny three-liner in the back of a newspaper. But we will say ten percent read and respond to your ad. That means you will get (we hope) about 1,000 replies. That is 1,000 who write or call and ask for more information.

They are not buyers yet. How many do you think will actually buy? If we use our ten percent formula (which is a very giving percentage), you might get 100 buyers. That figure sounds good.

But keep in mind that the ad cost over $1,000—*for one day*—and you had to pay to send those 1,000 responders some information. Will those 100 buyers net you a profit?

Classified Ads *Can* Work

1. Classified ads *do* work—sometimes—but usually after testing them in a small, inexpensive publication to see if the ad will work at all. Most classifieds fail because they are poorly worded or ask for too much. You cannot expect someone to send you $12.95 or more on the basis of a sales pitch in a three-line ad.

   According to Don Massey, of Don Massey Publications, asking for *any* money in a classified ad will not work today. He says 70 percent of his sales come from running a small ad offering free information, and then following up by sending the people who responded a sales letter about his small business.

2. You need consistency. When readers see your ad every day or every month, they begin to trust the ad and they will begin to respond to it. But you need money to keep the ads running a long, long time (at least three months).

3. Readers are overwhelmed. There are so many classifieds in every paper, every day, that getting yours noticed is a major hurdle. It is usually better to go one step up and take out a small display ad. At least you have a better opportunity to catch the reader's speeding eye.

When to Use a Classified

If you are offering a small ticket item—something that you sell for less than five dollars—you *may* find classified ads will do the trick for you. If you are offering something of far more value, a small classified ad does not give you enough space to create a sales argument. People will resist spending any money if all they know about your product or service is twenty words. You will have to give them a longer and stronger sales pitch. For that, you will need a larger ad.

If you want to generate leads, classifieds are powerful. This is called the *two-step* approach. You can flag down the prospects you want with a classified ad (*step one*), and then send them more information (the longer sales pitch) when they contact you (*step two*). This is the best use of a classified. It is the way for you to pinpoint the exact group of people who may be interested in your product or service. With a classified, you can "call them out" of the crowd.

How to Write a Classified Ad

Since by nature a classified ad is only a few lines and a handful of words, it ends up being a telegram. In order for your ad to get any responses, every word has to work. Here are some tips on how to make that happen:

1. Write an entire paragraph selling your product or service.

Write out exactly what you want to say to your prospect. Then go back and ruthlessly edit your words. If you wrote "Just call right now and we'll send you free information," you might cut that down to read "Call now—FREE info!" and lose nothing from your original intent.

2. Use a powerful headline.

Read Chapter Four on headlines again and then create a short but powerful grabber for your ad. One of the most successful ways to do this is to ask for the people you want. If you are taking an ad out in a magazine for chefs, begin the ad with something like "Attention: Chefs!" In other words, hone in and nail the prospects you want by addressing them directly. An ad I and many other guitar players recently responded to in a guitar magazine began with the words: "Guitar Players!" Make these headlines **bold face.**

3. Offer the key benefit right away.

If you are offering something free, say so. If you have a new book or tape or service or product, say so. The trick is to spell out how your item will help the reader. If your new system, for example, will help people save money on their taxes, say so: "Attention: Chefs! Save money on taxes with new accounting system!"

4. Ask for action.

You will *always* want your classified ad readers to do something. Have them write, call, or fax by telling them to write, call, or fax. And be sure you give them the information they need to do it.

5. Use dashes.

I like dashes because they are like arrows—they lead your eyes to the next word—or phrase—and speed up reading. It is a trick few know to help make your ad stand out—and look more visually attractive.

6. Use a symbol.

Classifieds typically have only words. You can make yours stand out by using a graphic—a tiny illustration or photo that is relevant to your ad. If you are running a small restaurant, you might run a picture of your restaurant or one of your popular dishes, inside the classified ad. Obviously this will increase the cost for your ad, but it will also increase the number of people who see it.

7. Use a border.

Most classified ads do not have borders. If you can put a heavy dashed line around your ad, it will leap off of the page.

8. Use the six most powerful words in mail order copy: *Free, New, Amazing, Now, How To,* **and** *Easy.*

Weave them into your classified ad for powerful results and high reader interest.

Classified Ad Examples

Here are a few classifieds that have been very successful. Note how they all still follow the famous AIDA formula: they get attention, generate interest and desire, and then call for action.

GUITARISTS—GET THE MENTAL EDGE! AMAZING new technique unleashes the MASTER GUITARIST INSIDE YOU! Increase **speed, focus, accuracy, and creativity.** ALL STYLES. Send $15 for audiocassette to **VAN ZEN PUBLISHING,** 8440 Fountain Ave, Suite 207, W. Hollywood, CA 90069. (213) 654-2610.

GET PAID TO WRITE YOUR BOOK. Major NY publishers now paying $5,000–$10,000 advances for nonfiction manuscripts. New authors welcome. Free information. CTC, Dept JV10, 22 E. Quackenbush Ave, Dumont, NJ 07628.

NO REJECTION SLIPS! Make homemade booklets. Mine have earned me $635,043. Money never stops. Write Don Massey, 507 Oak Drive, Friendswood, TX 77546.

Action Point

When used carefully, classified ads can work for your business product or service. Follow the guidelines in **Worksheet 13** as you write a classified ad that will get responses.

Worksheet 13

Writing a Classified Ad That Will Have Results

1. What do you want the ad to do—make a sale or generate a lead?

   _____

2. Write out a paragraph, even a whole page, to get someone to do what you want.

   _____

   _____

   _____

   _____

   _____

3. Now edit those lines and tighten your copy. Remember, a classified ad is usually (but not always) only a few lines and a dozen or so words. Also remember that you are paying for this ad *by the word*.

   _____

   _____

4. Create a short but catchy headline to lead off your ad. You might want to go back to Chapter Four on headlines and work through the worksheet there.

   _____

   _____

5. Have you given a key benefit? Be sure your ad has a benefit in it for your prospects. In other words, why should they respond? What is in it for them? What is your news that should excite your prospects?

   _____

   _____

   _____

   _____

6. Have you asked for action—and given the means to do it? Remember to tell the reader what to do and give the information needed to do it.

_____

_____

7. Can you improve the ad by tightening sentences, using dashes, or adding a graphic? How else can you make it more appealing and to the point?

_____

_____

_____

_____

8. Can you test the ad by running it in a small, inexpensive publication first? (If it works there, take it to a bigger magazine or newspaper. If it does not work, change the headline and try again.)

_____

_____

9. Now write your complete classified ad here:

_____

_____

_____

10. How can you make use of the six most powerful mail order words?

_____

_____

_____

11. Finally, pretend you are about to send the above ad as a telegram to the planet Mars and NASA is going to charge you $3,000.00 a word. Can you tighten your ad even more and still get your message across? (Instead of writing "ATTENTION: MARTIANS!" you might shorten it to say "MARTIANS!" and save yourself $3,000.00) Write your revised ad here:

_____

_____

_____

Chapter Ten

How to Win in the Yellow Pages

Read this information . . .	**. . . complete this Action Point**
Yellow Pages Tips	Worksheet 14: Designing or Improving Your Yellow Pages Ad

Most of my clients are small business owners. Whenever I get a chance to, I ask the question, "How do people hear about you?" The most common answer is "word of mouth." But one day I heard something different. "Word of mouth and my yellow pages ad," said Rodney Kamdar, owner of M & M Vacuum Company. "Those are about the only ways people hear about me."

Kamdar opened the big yellow pages on his desk. Among all the one-line listings and display ads for vacuum repairs, there was Kamdar's winner. "I'm proud of that ad," he said. "I designed it myself."

While all the other ads blended together because they looked so alike, Kamdar's was different. "Everyone else puts a regular line border around the ad," he explained. "I wanted to be different so I put stars around my ad."

Though the stars (* * * * * * * * *) were not as eye-catching as a bold dashed line might be (- - - - - - - - -), they certainly made his ad stand out among his competitors' ads.

"I also knew that people want to know what kind of vacuums I can fix," Kamdar continued. "So I listed all the makes and models in my ad. People look at the ad and instantly know I can help them. Once they come in, I serve them right and charm them into coming back again and again. They also tell all their friends, and that gets the word of mouth going."

Kamdar is on the right track and his small business is doing well. He knows two facts that help make him a success:

- Anyone who is looking in the yellow pages is ready to buy today. (That is why they picked up the directory. They have a need *right now*.)

- The bigger and better ads will get the most business. (One study reports that a display ad in the yellow pages will get up to 65 percent more business than a line listing.)

Just about every small business can justify being in the yellow pages. But how do you place an ad there that does not disappear? How do you create an ad that makes all those ready-to-buy people call *you*?

Yellow Pages Tips

Here are some guidelines for creating and placing an ad in the phone book that will get you the most results.

1. Be different.

All of the principles we have talked about apply when creating a yellow pages ad. This point is simply a reminder to get *attention* as fast as you can. You do not want to be silly or cute or clever, but you do want the appropriate attention of the people who are looking for someone like you. Nearly everyone listed in the yellow pages will state their name and give their number. You should be different. One smart way to do this is to have a headline that attracts the people you want. If you are a foot doctor, a bold headline that says "Sore Feet?" should grab your prospects. If you are a mechanic, you might begin with "Warning: Read This Before You Call *Any* Mechanic!"

2. Focus on direct benefits.

People looking in the yellow pages have a problem or need or desire. They do not want to see an ad that says "Kamdar's the Best!" because that means nothing to them. But they *do* want to see an ad that says "I Fix *All* Vacuums!" You may be running a cleaning service. A headline with your name will mean little. But saying "We Clean the Worst Messes" will offer a direct benefit.

3. Use a border.

Most advertisers are satisfied with a line listing (just your name and number) in the phone book. It is worth it to have a slightly larger display ad, mainly because it will get more attention. And to help insure that you get noticed, use a fancy border. Stars will work. So will a heavy bold line. My personal preference is a dashed-coupon look. But you can also be creative. A plumber might have a border made of pipes; a baker might have one made of donuts.

4. Offer something free.

As always, "Free" is the most powerful word in advertising. If you want people to call your swimming pool installation service, offer them an initial consultation free. If you run a business selling security systems, maybe offer to install one for thirty days so people can get the feel of what it is like to sleep in safety.

5. Give information.

Your name and phone number are not enough for most potential callers. They want to know what you can do (that is why Kamdar listed all the vacuums he can fix) and they want to know where you are (so give your location—even a small map). Imagine what questions a new prospect might have and try to answer them in your ad.

6. Be specific.

"I fix all cars" is not as powerful or persuasive or believable as "I fix all American cars" or "I specialize in Fords." Saying you give "great service" means *nothing*. *How* is your service great?

7. Run your ad as an advertorial or letter.

Again, the three types of ads talked about in Chapter Three will work in the yellow pages, too.

8. A good name helps.

A good company name can help you for two reasons:

- If your name begins with an early letter in the alphabet, your ad will be closer to the front of all the listings in your section. (Awareness Publications, for example, will get listed closer to the front in the publishers category.) When people look in your section, they will always see the first listings there before they start to scan them all.
- A good name can describe what you do. "Vacuum Repairs" says a lot more than "Kamdar Incorporated."

9. Put your phone number on the bottom.

People tend to read ads from left to right and top to bottom. They *expect* to see your phone number in the bottom third of your ad. Put it there.

10. Avoid photos.

While photos may help your ad in other situations, they typically do not help you in the yellow pages. The main reason is that the pictures often do not reproduce very well. You are better off with a line drawing or some other type of art work.

11. Avoid color.

Again, the yellow pages are a special breed. While color may help you in other situations, here it may not. The most common extra color used by the phone company is red, but studies show it is not worth the extra expense—which can be up to 50 percent more! Stick to black and white.

12. Get inspired by other ads.

Thumb through your local yellow pages. Better yet, visit your nearest library and thumb through directories from other cities, especially major ones in other states. Look for ads that get your attention and draw you in. How was the ad designed? What grabbed you? Discover what they are doing that works and then use that knowledge to design an ad for your small business. It is often a good idea to call the owner of the ad and ask them how the ad is doing. An ad that you think is clever may turn out to be a bomb. Get all the facts, then make your own ad.

13. Check out the directory.

Be sure you are in the right yellow pages. The phone company has many competitors. You want your ad to run in the directory that the phone company distributes to its customers.

14. Be under the right heading.

When people want your service, what section will they look under in the yellow pages? That is where you want to be.

 ## *Action Point*

You can design or improve your own yellow pages ad by following this chapter's guidelines. Use **Worksheet 14** as a checklist to review your current ad or a guide for designing a new ad.

Worksheet 14

Designing or Improving Your Yellow Pages Ad

1. Look at the ads of your competitors. What are they doing that gets attention and urges people to call them? _____
   _____
   _____

2. Look at the ads from other businesses in other categories. Which ads stand out? Why?_____
   _____
   _____

3. Look at ads from other businesses in other cities. Which ads seem to work? Why? _____
   _____
   _____

4. How can you make your ad different?_____
   _____
   _____

5. What border can you use to grab attention?_____
   _____
   _____

6. Have you given helpful and complete information?_____
   _____
   _____

7. Is your ad large enough to be seen among all the other ads in your section? _____
   _____
   _____

Chapter Eleven

How to Create Radio and Television Ads That Work

Your small business—no matter what it is—can probably benefit from radio and television advertising. Consider these facts:

- Radio is heard by 96.1 percent of everyone over the age of twelve—about 200,000,000 people a week!
- Network television is beamed into 98 percent of all U.S. households!

Clearly there is tremendous opportunity to use these media to tell people about your product or service. But there are also a few dangers.

Danger One

You cannot be cute or clever and expect your commercials to work. Advertising on radio or TV—as anywhere else—is supposed to do only one thing: Sell! David Deutsch, in *Million Dollar Marketing Secrets*, reveals the following:

- Chevrolet's "Heartbeat of America" TV campaign won praise but did not increase sales.
- The popular campaign "It's not nice to fool Mother Nature," was so ineffective the margarine company behind it is now out of business.
- The entertaining TV ads to sell batteries with the drum-beating pink rabbit have never worked because few viewers can remember whether the ad was for Duracell or Energizer batteries! (They keep running the ads because the company is hoping the public will catch on!)

The moral? Make every ad you do work *for you* by designing it to sell your small business product or service. Focus on what you can do for people and not on how clever you can be. Big businesses (like Chevrolet) might be able to afford to lose money on advertising that entertains but does not sell; you cannot.

Danger Two

Radio and TV ads can be expensive. According to Andrew Cohen, a New York ad consultant, a complete TV "infomercial" can run anywhere from $150,000 to $750,000. That is just to produce the tape. If you create the commercial yourself on 16mm film with a small camera, you can bring the cost down to under $20,000 or even a lot less. Still, you have to pay the station's fees on top of those production costs.

While rates vary from station to station and state to state, the price to air an ad can be staggering. Prime time on cable can run anywhere from $35 to $6,000 a minute. That is why many small business owners use this form of advertising as a last resort.

One way around this is to only advertise with tightly focused stations. For example, a cable TV show that reaches your market might be a good choice. The point is, seriously consider all angles before buying any radio or TV time. Call your local stations and let them tell you about their fees, services, and audiences. Then sift through all the information and make a rational decision.

The Secret Weapon of Radio and TV

In print ads, you are limited to the power of the words on the page. While an experienced copywriter can weave words into a nuclear arrangement and help sell your goods, that copywriter is still boxed in. A print ad can only carry words and images to make the sale.

Radio and TV, however, give you the means to engage people's other senses. You can involve listeners and viewers with sounds, lights, colors, images, and other sensations. You can demonstrate your product or service and give people a very real feel for what you have to offer. For example:

- A restaurant can *show* a mouth-watering steak in a TV ad and get people hungry for it. On radio you can *hear* the sizzle.

- A print shop can show flyers, brochures, business cards, and anything else being printed. The viewer can *see* the operation right on TV and get a sense of what you and your staff are like. On radio, you can talk about your services and even have real customers talk about their experiences with you so listeners *hear* your message.

The secret weapon of radio and TV ads is *life*. With radio and TV, you can almost put your potential customers and clients into your business. You are only limited by your imagination. You can take a small video camera virtually anywhere to get the look you want; you can use sound effects on radio to lead people to see whatever you want them to see. Radio and TV, in short, open up a whole new world of possibilities for you.

Radio Works, Too!

Most people are convinced television commercials will get results. But they are not so sure about radio. "Isn't it just a supportive tool?" "Isn't it something to use to reinforce your print and TV ads?"

Yes. *And* you can create direct response radio commercials that get results. The trick is in focusing on the offer, giving reasons to act today, and telling people to call now. Bob Schulberg, in *Radio Advertising*, gives the following proof of radio's power:

- Tens of thousands of radio listeners called to ask for a brochure about Australia after hearing Paul Hogan suggest they do so. (Hogan is a celebrity *and* an expert, since he is a movie star *and* from Australia.)
- Chicago's WBBM/Newsradio posted an on-air question relating to city government and received 30,000 phone calls in one day! (Proving that ads that involve people work.)
- In a two-week, one-station, one-market test, the state of Alaska received close to 6,000 phone requests for its travel brochure.

Radio, like TV, can work for you, too.

The Basic Formula

Good direct response radio and TV ads follow a basic formula. It is surprisingly similar to the AIDA (Attention–Interest–Desire–Action) formula. While the time you spend in each section may vary depending on your budget, the basic structure is usually the same.

Attention

The first one to five seconds have to grab your prospects or else they will switch channels. This is the same as in any print ad, where the headline and/or illustration have to stop your readers on the spot, or else they will run on rather than read on. This section is called the *holder* because it is designed to hold viewers and listeners so they will hear or see the rest of your commercial.

Premise

This section (often fifteen seconds long) is designed to create desire. This is where you describe what you are selling or offering. Very often you will hear someone in a good ad say, "You can have this set of (whatever) absolutely free, but first let me tell you about. . . ." You are being pulled into the commercial with the promise of more. This is the section where you wave a carrot in front of your prospects, telling them they can have it *if* they listen to all of your commercial.

Product

This section is sometimes up to thirty seconds long. This is where you create interest and deepen desire by demonstrating your product or service. The key word is *demonstrate*. Find a way to show your product or service in action. A famous TV ad to sell knives always showed those knives chopping and dicing, not just sitting in a display box. Another famous ad, this one designed to sell books, showed pictures of cowboys and had western music in the background to help viewers see and feel the essence of the books.

Ordering

In the last fifteen seconds of the ad, all the information needed for a person to order or set an appointment with you is given. This is the action stage of a good ad. You end your ad by asking people to order from you, or to call you, and giving them all the details they need. Your phone number, for example, should be on the screen for at least one third of your ad. You want people to have time to see it and write it down. And without it, most people will not do anything.

While the basic structure of a good TV or radio ad follows the AIDA formula, you should also upgrade this formula with the six key points talked about in Chapter Two. For example, you do not just want anyone's attention. You want to reach the people most likely to be interested in your small business. In other words, you want appropriate attention, which is part of those six keys for creating ads that work.

You Are Not a Clown

One of the biggest mistakes in TV and radio commercials is thinking you have to be humorous. While humor *can* help get your message across, it is probably the most dangerous strategy you could ever try.

> If you were invited into a customer's inner sanctum for the purpose of motivating a buying action, would you use precious seconds to tell a joke, mime, sing a song, or entertain with a brass band? Or would you get right down to the business of selling? Isn't it logical that you would take the allotted time to set forth the problems the customer may have relative to the service the product performs and then explain how your product solves those problems?
>
> —Al Eicoff, *Eicoff on Broadcast Direct Marketing*

Your product or service helps people in some way. Your radio or TV ad should focus on that benefit. Communicate *what is in it for the customer* and you will create a commercial that sells. You are only allowed a few seconds in your customer's home. Are you going to use that priceless time to joke around or *sell*?

Tips on Creating Winning Commercials

Here are some guidelines for creating radio and television ads that help sell your small business:

1. Get attention.

Again, if you do not hold your audience, they will not hear the rest of your message. A common way to get attention is to focus on the problem. "Can't lose weight?" "Can't get those stains out?" "Worried about medical insurance?" Think about your prospects and give them something new, useful, surprising, or different. Your goal is to reach the most people who would be *interested* in your service with the most *relevant hook* you can create.

2. Be simple and direct.

If your ad is clumsy or hard to follow, or so "information rich" that it is disorienting, people will zap you off the air with a touch of a button. Speak to people sincerely and simply. One popular TV ad for an attorney simply has the man sitting on his desk in his office, talking to the camera.

3. Create trust.

Again, this is a concern of every type of ad. If people do not believe you, they will not call you. If your ad looks unbelievable, prospects will not trust you. Testimonials work well here. Satisfied customers talking to viewers and listeners is a tried and true method of creating trust. Guarantees, of course, should *always* be in your ad.

4. Be original.

If your commercial looks like everyone else's or anyone else's ad, people will make the snap judgment they have already seen it and they will tune you out. Your ad should look alive and new so people want to see it. You do not have to be fancy or too creative to accomplish this. Simply tell your message and you will stand out in the crowd. One furniture store owner runs his TV ads with him standing beside a bed or a sofa and talking about it. He ends every ad by jumping in the air and saying "Gallery Furniture saves you money!" That ending is just different enough to make his ad original and his small business (now a *large* business) memorable.

5. Be personal.

Though thousands or more may see or hear your commercial, each person hears it or sees it personally. Speak to one person and you will capture the hearts of all viewers and listeners. Speak to that individual's interests and desires, hopes and dreams. Pretend you knocked on the door and you were invited into the living room to deliver your message. In effect, that is what radio and TV lets you do.

6. Motivate!

Your ad should follow a natural flow that leads to what you want your prospects to do. Every step of your commercial should walk people through a process to ordering from you or calling you. From getting their attention, through generating excitement for your small business, to finally calling you, your ad should be designed to get a particular result. While some large businesses might be able to afford the luxury of spending lots of money to sell an image to the public, as a small business you should be going for a more direct sell.

7. Answer all key questions.

If you leave something important unanswered, people will not call you. Your prospects have to know all the answers now, or be persuaded to call to learn more. Either way, your commercial has to give people all the information they need.

8. Make it easy to order.

Your telephone number should be on the screen *at least* fifteen seconds so people can write it down. It should be repeated often on radio. And avoid fancy mnemonic tricks (like "Call Joe-BOOK") because people often forget them (thinking they will remember them). If you insist on using a name for your number, *also* give the number. And if you take credit cards, show the cards on your screen or name them in your radio ads.

9. Demonstrate!

Your commercial should bring your product or service to life. There are many ways to do this. You can show the product in use; you can show a before-and-after situation where your product made the difference; you can create a torture test where your product is put through every tough situation and yet survives; you can show a problem and then show how your service solved it. The point is to make your prospects *feel* what your small business can do for them.

10. Choose the airing carefully.

Too many people air their radio and TV ads in the wrong places and at the wrong times. Prime time is usually *not* the best time for your ad (though, ironically, it is the most expensive). Studies show that if you air your ad during off hours, you will get more people paying attention to your message *and* responding to it. People will get up out of their chairs and leave a low interest movie aired late at night to make a call to you, but they will not leave the Super Bowl.

Again, as with every type of ad, you want to reach the people who will be most interested in your product or service. What do your prospects watch on TV or listen to on the radio? Advertise where they are already gathered.

Sandra Stokes, a commercial director in Baton Rouge, says:

> You want high viewership in *your target market*. I currently produce commercials for social security disability and we air them during daytime programs because our target market is unemployed and known to sit at home and watch TV all day long!

11. Take the time.

Longer TV ads tend to sell better than shorter ones, mainly because you have a better chance to give a *complete* sales pitch for your small business. "Infomercials" are TV ads, usually thirty minutes long, designed to give all the information you need to make a sale. As with a print ad, you do not want to make your ad long just to get it long; every word should work to get your prospects to call you. (Short commercials work, too, but they better *sell.*)

12. Be honest.

You cannot mislead prospects in *any* ads, of course, because doing so is illegal. According to Kenneth Roman and Jane Maas in *The New How to Advertise*, "The advertising will be judged not by what it says, but by what the consumer *thinks* it says." Your commercials should be clear, direct, and truthful. This is particularly important if you are selling food. Words like "fresh" and "light" and "fat-free" are regulated by the Food and Drug Administration.

13. Show life.

Emotion sells. One way of involving a viewer or listener is to have two people argue over the merits of your business. This "slice of life" type of commercial is very effective because it stirs emotions while selling your product or service. Example: Neighbor Joe wants to prove to neighbor Ted that Gulf Coast Security Systems is the best for home protection. They argue about it until Joe somehow proves to Ted that yes, indeed, Gulf Coast is pretty darn impressive after all.

14. Give your name!

Anything aired is quickly forgotten *forever* once it is off the air. Help your prospects remember you by telling them who you are quickly and often.

15. Frequency is key.

You cannot run a radio or TV ad once and expect results. You have to air it several times a day and nearly every day of the week. But give your ad a break now and then. Run it for five weeks, then take a week off, then air it again.

16. Write your own—or hire a pro.

Do not let the radio or TV station write your ad, even if they offer to do it for free. Why? You will end up with a commercial similar to everyone else. Either create your own commercial, using the principles in this book, or hire a copywriter to write it for you. There is nothing wrong with using the station's equipment, however. It could be an easy way for you to create your own commercial. And some stations will even come to your place of business and record your commercial for you!

17. Show people.

People are interested in people. Have real people on the air or on camera testifying to their experiences with your business. You should also go on the air so people get to "know" who you are.

18. Avoid comparisons.

You almost never have to talk about your competition to prove you are better than them. Besides, you do not want to give them the free publicity. Focus on the benefits people get from *your* product or service.

19. Use "sound design."

While music may help create a mood, it typically does not help sell anything. Besides that, music is copyrighted and to use it you would have to pay a royalty. Jingles almost never sell anything. But the clever use of sound can help get your message across. For example, seeing eggs cooking while you hear them sizzle and crack is very involving and memorable. Use sound to help make your ad more colorful, alive, and unforgettable.

20. Be single-minded.

What is your basic offer? Your commercial should be working to get across one point in the most effective and dramatic way possible. If someone (a copywriter or fellow employee) presents you with a *storyboard* (a sketch, frame by frame, of a commercial), look for the basic selling message. There should be only one. You do not want to complicate or confuse people. Commercials that are too entertaining can cloud your basic sales message.

21. Use celebrities.

While the use of celebrities in print ads is not effective, it does seem to help grab and hold attention in radio and TV ads. You may not be able to afford Madonna, but there are many recognizable actors and actresses who will advertise your business for a relatively small fee. You can contact them through their agents, the reference section of your library, or in directories such as Michael Levine's *The Address Book*.

22. Run it near the news.

Murray Raphel, in *Customerization*, says he always tries to buy *adjacencies* to the news broadcasts. An adjacency is a commercial aired before, during, or after a news broadcast; it is run adjacent to it. Most people tend to listen to the news and will also hear or see your commercial.

23. Use tight close-ups in TV.

Close-ups of a person talking to the camera are very effective. For a small business, this one-on-one type of face-to-face selling is very effective. The viewer gets the feeling of being spoken to *directly*. This is also cheaper than using props or expensive settings.

24. Use silence.

People expect sound on their TV or radio. That is why they turned it on. Stop that noise for a micro-second and you will get attention. Consider the famous ad that said, "We make money the old fashioned way." *Silence.* "We earn it." The silence adds impact to the next line. But do not leave the silence there too long or people will think the station went off the air!

25. Wheel and deal.

Radio and TV air time can be sold in various packages and at various times and in various amounts. Negotiate. Tell the station salesperson you have $1,000 (or whatever) budgeted for a six-week ad campaign. How much air time can they give you? Will they give it when your target audience is watching? Will they produce the commercial for you, too? Might they also run a news story on your business?

 Action Point

Your can use **Worksheet 15** as a blueprint to help you design and create an effective radio or television commercial. Remember to use the questions as prompts, not rules. Let your mind go and brainstorm different ways you can use the airwaves to reach—and sell—your prospects.

Worksheet 15

Design and Create an Effective Radio or TV Commercial

1. Who are you trying to reach? _____

2. What do they listen to or watch?_____

3. What do you want them to do? _____

4. How can you get their attention and hold it?_____
   _____
   _____

5. What can you offer them to hold their interest? _____
   _____

6. How can you demonstrate your product or service?
   _____
   _____

7. What people do you have lined up to give testimonials?
   _____
   _____

8. Do you have a solid guarantee? _____

9. If you were visiting one new prospect and wanted to sell that prospect on your small business, what would you say to that person?
   _____
   _____
   _____
   _____

10. Have you made ordering or calling you easy?_____

11. How can you use sound effects to make people hear and understand your message? _____

_____

_____

_____

12. What can you show people visually to help them understand your service? _____

_____

13. What is in it for the customers? Why should they call you?

_____

_____

14. Why should they call you NOW? _____

_____

_____

15. How else can you make your commercial involving and informative?

_____

_____

Chapter Twelve
34 Ways to Increase Responses to Your Ads

Read this information . . .	. . . complete this Action Point
Room for Improvement in Any Ad	Worksheet 16: Improving Your Successful Ad

One day a financial consultant asked me to look at his ad. He said it was not doing very well. I could see why. His ad had no reason for being other than to please his own ego. The headline was not intriguing. There was no news. Or a story. There was no offer or any reason to call him. All the ad did was give his name and list his services.

We sat down and I began to tell him all the ways he could improve his ad. His eyes widened as he saw all the possibilities he had been missing. Like most people running a small business, he was not aware of what he was doing wrong—or how easily his problem could be transformed.

Now that you have read this far, the ad *you* create will be far more powerful than my client's. Still, there is always room for improvement. With that in mind, here are several ways you can dramatically increase the responses you are getting from any ad.

Room for Improvement in Any Ad

1. Add personality.

When Norman Rockwell was hired to create a drawing of a museum, he shocked the advertising agency by adding a drawing of the museum's founder, too. What everyone quickly realized was the character brought the building to life—and helped that small tourist attraction pull in more business than ever before. Remember, people are interested in people. Add a person to your ad and you add color and personality.

2. Add drama.

When David Ogilvy created a now-famous ad to sell shirts, he had the model wear an eye patch. That simple prop gave the whole ad drama. People seek excitement. When you create an ad that signals "There is a story here," people will stop and begin to read your copy.

3. Change the ad's size.

If you are running a small ad, make it bigger. As expected, studies prove that larger ads get more attention.

4. Change your headline.

People skim headlines to help them choose what they want to read. A different headline may get you more readers—and more people calling you.

5. Change the ad's location.

Though research suggests your ad's position on a page does not affect results, you do not want your ad buried on the page. See if you can run it on the front or back page of a section of a newspaper, or the front or back page of a magazine, which are places that cost more but which are also seen more. Or see if you can place your ad on the same page with regular editorial material in the paper or magazine. People reading a story will also see your ad.

6. Change the border.

One trick to get more readers is to place a heavy dashed line all around your ad, making it look like a coupon. Since we are all trained to look for coupons, the ad gets our attention. You can also experiment and try other types of borders. A heavy solid black line gets attention. A wavy, picture-frame type border also gets attention.

7. Mention a flaw.

A way to gain credibility is to admit a defect in your product or service. For example, one small business consultant said he wouldn't fly anywhere to help anybody. You had to come to him. Because he admitted he had an apparent weakness (fear of flying), people believed everything else he said. Far too many small business people just blow their own horn and say they are the greatest. Be honest. Add a weak point of your small business to your ad and people will believe everything else you say.

8. Offer something *free.*

The most powerful word in advertising is still "free." Offer a free booklet, book, tape, consultation, etc., to get potential customers into your door. The trick is to offer something relevant to you and your targeted customers. Do not offer season tickets to the opera if your small business has nothing to do with the opera.

9. Change the deadline.

People need a reason to act now—or they will not. Give a tighter deadline and you may encourage people to act. You might also try giving an extended deadline to see if that works any better.

10. Extend your guarantee.

If you offer a 30-day guarantee, change it to a 60-day guarantee. If you offer a 60-day guarantee, consider changing it to a 90-day guarantee. People need to feel safe when buying from you. A guarantee helps ease their discomfort. An unlimited, no-questions-asked guarantee is best.

11. Answer the phone.

Recently I saw an ad for an answering service that made me call. But when I called, no one answered the phone! You will increase responses to your ad if you do what your ad claims. If you want people to fax you, be sure your fax machine is on. In short, do exactly what you say you will do in your ad! *Never* turn off your phone or FAX machine.

12. Fill the white space.

People still think lots of white space makes a good ad. Not necessarily! All you have to do is look at your newspaper. People buy it for news. How much white space do the editors leave? None! Learn from newspaper and magazine editors. If your headline is involving, people will read the story. If the story is well written and interests them, they will read every word—even if there is not any white space! Consider adding more copy to your ad. Remember that these words have to be interesting, otherwise you will bore people. One study revealed that adding facts to a small real estate ad *doubled* the number of calls it generated. Again, people want information of interest to them.

13. Change the type font.

Some people get too fancy with typefaces. You want your ad to be easy to read. If your type looks odd or hard to read, change it. The most common font for ads is Times Roman serif. Over 90 percent of all newspapers use this for their copy because it is so easy to read. Consider using one particular (and readable) font in all your ads to help get people accustomed to your advertising style.

14. Reverse type the headline.

You might get more readers if you put your headline in reverse type (white letters on a black background). But by all means do *not* set your whole ad that way, as it would be too hard to read.

15. Use a ragged right margin.

Studies show that people unconsciously use the ragged right side of the page (type that is uneven on the right margin) to help keep their place when they are reading. If you justify both sides of your ad copy, you will make the ad that much harder to read. Again, make everything easy for your customers and clients.

16. Show happiness.

You may have a nice picture in your ad, but you may get more responses if you try this: Show happiness. There was a study on all the Coca-Cola commercials and ads from the last 100 years and it found the one element all the successful ads had in common was *happiness*. Show smiling people and people associate good feelings with your product or service.

17. Run the ad where the buyers are.

Many people run their ads in the highest circulation periodicals they can find. Do not do this. You are not selling to "everybody." Target your prospects. Maybe your potential buyers are woodworkers. If so, you would be wiser to advertise in something all those carpenters are reading, which may not be a national or local paper. If you have a sports store, run your ad in the sports section of the paper. In other words, go fishing where the fish you want are swimming.

18. Run your ad longer.

You cannot expect an ad to run once and pull all the business you want. Studies prove people have to see your ad at least three to seven times before they feel comfortable enough to think you are real and it is okay to call you. Run your ad for at least three weeks in a newspaper, three months in a magazine.

19. Switch from papers to magazines.

A newspaper ad lasts one day; a magazine ad lasts one month— or longer. You will get more mileage out of one ad in a magazine that is read by your potential customers than you ever will with one newspaper ad.

20. Run an editorial-style ad.

This is one of the three formats we discussed earlier. It typically will get more readers than any other type of ad. If you are not running this kind, consider it to help increase your responses. Any business can create an advertorial. If a news story can be written about your business, then an advertorial can be written, too.

21. Take credit cards.

If you take credit cards, say so. Better yet, show that you do by printing the little credit card symbols at the bottom of your ad. You will get more replies if people know they can pay you with their credit cards. In fact, the more ways you can accept payment, the more replies you can get. Consider layaway, COD, multi-month payments, etc.

22. Add a color.

If you are running a black-and-white ad, consider adding one color. Though expensive, the extra color will attract more eyes to your ads—and possibly more buyers. Adding just one color can increase readers by 40 to 60 percent.

23. Change your illustration to a photo.

If you are using a line drawing or clip art in your ad, change to a photo. Pictures have more credibility and get more attention.

24. Involve your readers.

Your ad should involve your potential customers. Try a quiz or a contest. Think of a way to make your ad engaging. Just keep in mind that you want your ad to sell. One of the most popular sections of a newspaper is the crossword puzzle. You might design an ad that is a crossword puzzle. People will fill it out (which is very involving). To make it serve you, somehow tie in the puzzle to your business or service. You might ask readers to send in the puzzles, and then hold a drawing for the winner. The point is, *involve the reader* in your ad.

25. Add a coupon or gift certificate.

If you do not already have a coupon, add one. Ads with coupons are proven to get more responses than ads without coupons.

26. Change your offer.

Why should readers call you or hire you or buy from you? If you do not give them a good reason to contact you rather than your competitors, your ad may fail. Can you give readers part or all of your service free? Can you give them additional service, something extra, to urge them to call you? Can you give a better discount? Make a better offer and you will get better results.

27. Change your photo.

You may already have a nice photo in your ad, but test its power by changing the photo. See which photo pulls in more responses. In one ad use a photo of your product or your staff. The next time you run the ad, leave everything the same except the photo. Try a different one. Very often a different photo will increase your replies.

28. Add a border of white space.

Even if you already have a dashed line as your border, *add* a border of white space around it. This will help set off your ad from everything on the page. This does not conflict with suggestion Twelve because a border of white space goes outside and around your ad, not in it.

29. Make it eye easy.

Studies prove that an ad with a single central focus and a smooth sequence for the eye helps results. If you are trying to sell too much or make too many selling points, you will confuse and overwhelm people. If your ad is cluttered or hard to follow, you will lose readers. Use a strong headline, graphics that sell while leading the eyes, and use "helpers"—subheads, for example—to help readers see, grasp, and understand your ad's message. Start the copy of your ad with a *drop cap* letter (an oversized letter) to help people into your ad. This sentence began with a drop cap.

30. Add years in business.

Anything that adds credibility will help your ad. If you began your business in 1992, say "Established 1992." People want to know it is safe to do business with you. Something as small as a line about your years in operation can make a difference in your replies.

31. Advertise in respected places.

Where you advertise says a lot about your business. If you run an ad in a questionable or poorly-respected publication, you will be associated with that image. An ad in a well-regarded publication, read by your prospects, gives you authenticity. Consider the image the publication will give your business.

32. Use the "psychology of the second interest."

People bought Crackerjack to get the "free" surprise toy inside. People will buy a new picnic table just to get the "free" chairs they need. Offer something your prospects want for free if they buy something else, and you can increase responses by 10 to 50 percent. You have to spell out your terms to be legally safe. Be sure to say "Free *when you buy*. . . ." This technique is different from number Eight because here you will give something away only *when* your customers buy something.

33. Hold a sweepstakes.

You can increase your responses 35 to 100 percent—or more—with this method. This does not have to be a "million dollar" give-away, either. Offer a free trip, free gift, or free product in your own sweepstakes and you can draw in crowds. Simply make a deal with another business: You get their product at a discount to give as the prize and they get free advertising by being mentioned in your ads about the sweepstakes. State and county laws vary, so visit a consultant or attorney before designing any sweepstakes.

34. Give your prices.

People often do not respond to your ads because they do not know—and even fear—your prices. If they see that you have chairs for sale, they may be curious but talk themselves out of calling you by saying, "Oh, it probably costs too much for me." Give your prices and let the customer decide to visit or call you.

Action Point

Take an ad you have developed during the course of working through this book, or one you have run before. Improve it using one or more of the methods from this chapter. **Worksheet 16** will take you through each of the suggestions discussed in Chapter Twelve.

Worksheet 16

Improving Your Successful Ad

1. How can you add a personality to make your ad more human, appealing, and interesting? _____

2. How can you add drama?_____

3. Can you enlarge the ad? _____

4. What other headline can you test? _____

5. Where else can you run your ad? _____

6. What other border can you use? _____

7. What flaw or weakness can you mention in your ad to gain credibility for everything else you do? _____

8. What can you offer free?_____

9. Can you increase your deadline to encourage action? _____

10. Can you extend your guarantee?_____

11. Are you prepared to answer the phone and take appointments and handle the work the ad brings in for you?_____

12. Have you filled the white space with interesting copy? _____

13. Are you using a readable typeface? _____

14. Have you tried a reverse-type headline?_____

15. Does your copy have ragged right margins?_____

16. Does your ad show happy people?_____

17. What do your prospects read?_____

18. Can you run your ad longer? _____

19. Can you advertise in magazines? _____

20. Can you run an advertorial-style ad? _____

21. If you take credit cards, have you said so? _____

22. Can you add a color to your ad?_____

23. Instead of an illustration, can you run a photo? _____

24. How else can you make your ad *involve* readers?

_____
_____

25. Can you add a coupon to your ad? _____

26. What other offer can you make to entice people to call you?

_____

27. What other photo can you use in your ad?_____

28. Can you add a border of white space? _____

29. How can you make your ad's layout more visually attractive? _____

_____

30. Have you given your years in business? _____

31. Are you advertising in places your potential clients respect?_____

32. What can you offer free when they buy? _____

33. Can you create a sweepstakes? _____

34. Have you given your prices? _____

Chapter Thirteen

How to Check Your Final Ad

Read this information . . .	. . . complete this Action Point
The John Caples' Checklist	Worksheet 17: The Final Test Checklist

$\mathbf{B}$efore you pay to run your finished ad in a newspaper or magazine, or to air it on radio or television, how do you check it to be sure it is right? The only real way to test your ad is to actually run it and see what happens. But this is risky. As John Wanamaker said, "I know that half the money I spend on advertising is wasted; but I can never find out which half."

The John Caples' Checklist

Thanks to a legend in the advertising business, there *is* a way to double-check your ad before you let it out the door. The late John Caples was a genius at writing sales copy and creating ads that worked. He was also kind enough to record his insights for the rest of us. In one of his lesser-known books, *Making Ads Pay*, Caples revealed a seven-step formula for successful advertising. He wrote:

> This checklist is based on the results of hundreds of advertising tests. It is based on millions of dollars spent in experiments designed to find out what kind of advertising sells and what kind doesn't sell. The next time you prepare an ad or a commercial, put this checklist alongside of it.

 Action Point

Worksheet 17 is Caples' checklist with added commentary. Use it to give your ad the final test before you pay to run it.

Worksheet 17

The Final Test Checklist

1. Does your ad attract the **right audience**?
   Does your ad stop the *appropriate* people—the ones most likely to be interested in your product or service? Does your headline, photo, or opening grab the attention of your most likely prospects?

   _____

   _____

2. Does your ad **hold** the audience?
   You may have stopped them, but does your ad make them *stay*? The reader is itching to move on. Does your ad or commercial speak to that reader's interests, needs, hopes, or dreams? Does your ad maintain the attention it achieved?

   _____

   _____

3. Does your copy **create desire**?
   Do you promise benefits to the reader? Do you explain—in clear, easy, exciting, concrete terms—the advantages of your product or service? Do you reveal what the customer *will get*? Does your ad make that customer feel and want your service? Do you tell your customers what's in it for them?

   _____

   _____

4. Do you prove it is a **bargain**?
   Is your price lower than usual? Are you giving more service or adding more value than your competitors? Are you offering something no one else has? Are you offering a real deal and saying so in simple language?

   _____

   _____

5. Do you establish **confidence**?

   Or to put it the way Caples said it: "Prove it is *not* a *gyp*." You may have people interested in your ad. Now they are wondering if what you claim is really true. Dissolve their fears with testimonials, a guarantee, or any *proof* you have that it is safe to call you or order from you.

   _____

   _____

6. Do you make it **easy to act**?

   If you want your prospects to do something, have you *told them* what to do? Have you given them the information they need so they can do it? Have you made responding to your ad or commercial a snap?

   _____

   _____

7. Do you give your prospects a reason to **act at once**?

   Your potential customers may be ready to buy—but they will not unless you give them a *good reason* to act now. If your price is going up, say so. If supplies are limited, say so. If this is a limited time offer, say so. Have you given people a logical and believable reason to take you up on your offer right now, *this* minute?

   _____

   _____

Questions and Answers

How do I find out where to advertise?

First, learn more about your prospects. What do they read, watch, or listen to? *That* is where you should advertise. You can also look in the *Ayer Directory of Publications* for details on different media. Also check the *Standard Rate & Data Books*. Ask your library for assistance.

When do I stop advertising?

Never! Notice that Coca-Cola is still advertising—even though they are doing well. They advertise to *continue* doing well. You should, too.

If I am tired of my ad, can I change it?

If it is getting results, no. Henry Ford looked at an ad and said, "I'm tired of this campaign." The copywriter said, "Sir, this ad hasn't run yet." You may be tired of your ad before your prospects ever get a chance to notice it.

How much should I spend on advertising?

It depends on what you can afford. Advertising should be budgeted just like any other expense. Ask your accountant for help or visit the Small Business Administration (SBA) for assistance on determining what you can afford. One group of the SBA to contact is CORE (Committee of Retired Executives) or even Silver Foxes. Talk to anyone who has experience in your particular field of interest.

How do I figure how much advertising will cost me to get clients?

The most common way to calculate this is with a *cost per thousand* or CPM formula. This reveals how much it will cost you to reach 1,000 people through a particular avenue. In other words, if you are about to advertise in a magazine with a circulation of 24,000 readers and the ad cost is $720, the CPM would be $30. That means it costs you—in that publication—$30 to reach every 1,000 people. That is pretty cheap, and a smart investment if your prospects read that publication. You can figure the CPM for any ad by dividing the ad's cost in that publication by the circulation of that publication.

What results can I expect?

Great question! Unfortunately, there is not a great answer. Your results will depend on so many variables it is not funny. Besides the ad itself, and where you place it, there are outside influences you cannot control. If your ad appears on a rainy day, you may have fewer replies. If something big happens in the news, your ad probably will not get noticed. If your employees do not answer the phone when clients call, you will not get responses. There is no way to predict the results of any ad.

Who does the finished layout of my ad?

If you have a computer and the talent, you can do it. Or you can let the newspaper or magazine do it. Or you can hire a graphic artist. For radio and television, you can rent a studio and the professionals you need, or you can let the stations do it for you.

What if my ad fails?

Change the ad! Run it with a different headline. Are the results different? Now change the photo and see what happens. Change where you ran the ad, too. Keep testing each element in your ad until you discover the formula that works. Then do not change it.

What about new forms of advertising?

Whether you advertise by fax, video, billboard, cable, CD, computer bulletin boards, or carrier pigeons, your ads should follow the principles revealed in this book. How you deliver your ad may change, but how you prepare the ad should follow guidelines that do one thing: *Sell!*

Are advertising specialties of any value?

Mugs, pens, key chains, or whatever are very helpful as supportive advertising. In other words, if I give you a pen with my name and number printed on it, it probably will not sell you on my copywriting services. But it might *remind* you of me down the road. The trick to making novelty items like this work is to make them useful. You will use a pen and it fits with me being a writer. But a balloon is ridiculous. You might use a calendar or a key chain, but not a toy dinosaur. Try to give your clients something useful that reminds them of your business.

What is supportive advertising?

It is when you use one medium to support another one. If you have an ad in the local paper, you might create a ten-second radio commercial that says "See our ad in today's paper." The radio ad supports your print ad.

Glossary

AIDA: Famous "formula" for designing an ad layout. It stands for *A*ttention, *I*nterest, *D*esire, and *A*ction.

Advertising: Written, verbal, pictorial or graphic announcements of goods or services for sale, using time or space purchased by the advertiser.

Advertiser: The person or business who pays to run an advertisement.

Ad Specialties: Inexpensive items, such as mugs or pens, imprinted with the advertiser's name, often used as a promotional gift.

Advertorial: An ad designed to look like a newspaper or magazine article.

Believability: The degree of acceptance as truth of an ad's claims and contents.

Border: A rule used to outline an ad and set it apart from other ads or stories on a page.

Cable: Television paid for by subscription and transmitted by cable into households.

Camera-Ready Copy: An ad that is finished and ready to be photographed and reproduced.

Copy: The written portions of any type of ad.

Copywriter: The person who writes the advertising.

Coupons: A certificate or portion of an ad designed to be filled in and/or returned to the advertiser for a special discount or free item.

CPM: Mathematical formula for figuring the "cost per thousand," or what an ad in a particular medium cost to reach 1,000 people.

Classifieds: The section of a newspaper or magazine divided into the types of products or services sold.

Direct Mail Advertising: Ads sent through the mail to prospects.

Direct Response Advertising: Advertising that requires a response from the prospects receiving it.

Graphic Artist: The person who designs ad layout using illustrations, photos and/or copy.

Graphics: Illustrations or photos or any other visual devices used in ads.

Guarantee: The written commitment that a product or service will perform as specified or be replaced, repaired or the cost refunded.

Headline: The heading, usually a title, of an ad.

Holder: The opening of a radio or television ad designed to capture attention and "hold" the audience.

Image Advertising: Ads that strive to sell an image of a business more than a particular product or service.

Infomercial: A television or radio ad designed to look like a news story.

Key: A way of tracking responses to an ad, usually by adding a code number to a coupon.

Layout: How an ad is designed to look, usually a sketch to show the ad's intended content and structure.

List: The mailing list used in any direct mail advertising.

Leads: The people who respond to a particular ad who are now prospects for more sales.

Marketing: The business activities that determine the sales of goods or services, including but not limited to advertising.

Mailing List Broker: A specialist who makes arrangements for one company to make use of a list owned by another company.

Offer: The terms under which a specific product or service is promoted.

Open Letter Ad: An ad layout designed to look like a letter.

PAPA: A formula for designing an ad. Refers to *p*romise, *a*mplify, *p*roof, and *a*ction.

Public Relations: The process of influencing attitudes and opinions of a group of people in the interest of promoting a product or service.

Premium: An item offered free or at a nominal price as an inducement to buy or obtain for trial the advertised product or service.

Promotion: Any effort to create interest in the purchase of a particular product or service, often done with contests and sweepstakes.

Sales Letter: A letter on a company's letterhead designed and mailed to persuade prospects to respond.

Sound Design: The use of sound effects to generate moods in radio or television ads.

Spot: Any brief commercial on radio or television.

Storyboard: A layout of a television commercial that uses illustrations to show the sequence of the ad.

Supportive Advertising: The use of one advertising medium to reinforce ads in another advertising medium.

Testimonial: An endorsement for a product or service by a satisfied customer or client.

Testing: An effort to discover which ads work best by keying ads and tracking results.

Time Discount: A rate reduction for advertisers who make quantity purchases of broadcast time.

Type: The particular font, or style, of printed characters (numbers and letters, etc.).

USP: The original and unique benefit, or unique selling proposition, claimed for an advertised product or service.

Bibliography

Antin, Tony. *Great Print Advertising* (New York: Wiley, 1993).

Bates, Charles Austin. *Good Advertising* (New York: Holmes, 1896).

Bly, Robert W. *Advertising Manager's Handbook* (Englewood Cliffs, NJ: Prentice-Hall, 1993).

Bly, Robert W. *The Copywriter's Handbook* (New York: Dodd, Mead, 1985).

Caples, John. *Making Ads Pay* (New York: Dover, 1957).

Caples, John. *Tested Advertising Methods* (Englewood Cliffs, NJ: Prentice-Hall, 1974).

Caples, John. *How to Make Your Advertising Make Money* (Englewood Cliffs, NJ: Prentice-Hall, 1983).

Deutsch, David. *Million Dollar Marketing Secrets* (Richmond, VA: DLA Publications, 1992).

Eicoff, Al. *Eicoff on Broadcast Direct Marketing* (Chicago: NTC Business Books, 1988).

Ferguson, Bill. *How to Heal a Painful Relationship* (Houston: Return to the Heart, 1990).

Fisher, Donna. *Power Networking* (Houston: MountainHarbour Publications, 1992).

Garn, Roy. *The Magic Power of Emotional Appeal* (Englewood Cliffs, NJ: Prentice-Hall, 1960).

Hopkins, Claude. *Scientific Advertising* (Chicago: NTC Business Books, 1990).

Levine, Michael. *The Address Book* (New York: Putnam, 1993).

Lewis, Herschell Gordon. *How to Make Your Advertising Twice as Effective at Half the Cost* (Chicago: Bonus Books, 1990).

Mackay, Harvey. *Swim with the Sharks without Being Eaten Alive* (New York: Ballantine, 1988).

Mantice, Jim. *Slash Your Advertising Costs Now* (Chicago: Dartnell, 1991).

Ogilvy, David. *Confessions of an Advertising Man* (New York: Macmillan, 1987).

Ogilvy, David. *Ogilvy on Advertising* (New York: Vintage, 1985).

Raphel, Murray and Considine, Ray. *The Great Brain Robbery* (Atlantic City: Raphel Publishing, 1987).

Raphel, Murray and Erdman, Ken. *The Do-It-Yourself Direct Mail Handbook* (Atlantic City: Raphel Publishing, 1992).

Raphel, Murray. *Customerization* (Atlantic City: Raphel Publishing, 1993).

Roman, Kenneth and Maas, Jane. *The New How to Advertise* (New York: St. Martin's Press, 1992).

Ryan, Christopher. *The Master Marketer* (Rockville, MD: IdeaWorks Publishing, 1993).

Schulberg, Bob. *Radio Advertising* (Chicago: NTC Business Books, 1990).

Schwab, Victor. *How to Write a Good Advertisement* (Hollywood: Wilshire, 1962).

Vitale, Joe. *Turbocharge Your Writing!* (Houston: Awareness Publications, 1988).

Vitale, Joe. *The Seven Lost Secrets of Success* (Ashland, Ohio: VistaTron, 1992).

Vitale, Joe and McCann, Ron. *The Joy of Service!* (Houston: SIS Publications, 1989).

About the Author

JOE VITALE, President of the Joe Vitale Agency in Houston, is a speaker, marketing consultant, author, and copywriter.

He has written ads, sales letters, and brochures for a wide variety of small businesses across the country. Mr. Vitale's background in direct selling (cars, software, and other top-of-the-line products), mail order, and as a personal growth counselor helps him write record-breaking copy. One of his letters is currently achieving a 97 percent response rate.

Mr. Vitale is the author of several books, including *The Seven Lost Secrets of Success* (VistaTron, 1992), *Turbocharge Your Writing!* (Awareness Publications, 1988) and *The Joy of Service!* with Ron McCann (SIS Publications, 1989).

To receive information about Joe Vitale's writing and marketing services, talks and seminars, or books and tapes, contact:

Joe Vitale
P.O. Box 300792, Dept. A12
Houston, TX 77230-0792
Office: (713) 999-1110
FAX: (713) 999-1313

Index

TITLES OF INTEREST IN
ADVERTISING, SALES PROMOTION, AND PUBLIC RELATIONS

INTEGRATED MARKETING COMMUNICATIONS, by Don E. Schultz, Stanley I. Tannenbaum, and Robert F. Lauterborn

PROMOTIONAL MARKETING: IDEAS AND TECHNIQUES FOR SUCCESS IN SALES PROMOTION, by William A. Robinson and Christine Hauri

SALES PROMOTION ESSENTIALS, Second Edition, by Don E. Schultz, William A. Robinson, and Lisa Petrison

SALES PROMOTION MANAGEMENT, by Don E. Schultz and William A. Robinson

BEST SALES PROMOTIONS, Sixth Edition, by William A. Robinson

SUCCESSFUL DIRECT MARKETING METHODS, Fourth Edition, by Bob Stone

CREATIVE STRATEGY IN DIRECT MARKETING, by Susan K. Jones

PROFITABLE DIRECT MARKETING, Second Edition, by Jim Kobs

STRATEGIC DATABASE MARKETING, by Robert R. Jackson and Paul Wang

SECRETS OF SUCCESSFUL DIRECT MAIL, by Richard V. Benson

SUCCESSFUL ADVERTISING RESEARCH METHODS, by Jack Haskins and Alice Kendrick

CASES IN ADVERTISING MANAGEMENT, edited by Terence Nevett

STRATEGIC ADVERTISING CAMPAIGNS, Third Edition, by Don E. Schultz

WHICH AD PULLED BEST? Sixth Edition, by Philip Ward Burton and Scott C. Purvis

STRATEGY IN ADVERTISING, Second Edition, by Leo Bogart

HOW TO PRODUCE CREATIVE ADVERTISING, by Ann Keding and Thomas Bivins

ADVERTISING IN SOCIETY, by Roxanne Hovland and Gary Wilcox

ESSENTIALS OF ADVERTISING STRATEGY, Second Edition, by Don E. Schultz and Stanley I. Tannenbaum

CHOOSING AND WORKING WITH YOUR ADVERTISING AGENCY, Second Edition, by William A. Weilbacher

CHOOSING AND WORKING WITH YOUR PUBLIC RELATIONS FIRM, by Thomas L. Harris

THE ADVERTISING AGENCY BUSINESS, Second Edition, by Herbert S. Gardner, Jr.

BUSINESS TO BUSINESS ADVERTISING, by Charles H. Patti, Steven W. Hartley and Susan L. Kennedy

BUSINESS TO BUSINESS MARKETING COMMUNICATIONS, by Fred Messner

BUSINESS TO BUSINESS DIRECT MARKETING, by Robert Bly

THE PUBLICITY HANDBOOK, by David Yale

HANDBOOK FOR PUBLIC RELATIONS WRITING, by Thomas Bivins

POWER PUBLIC RELATIONS, by Leonard Saffir and Jack Tarrant

THE DICTIONARY OF ADVERTISING, by Laurance Urdang

THE ADVERTISING PORTFOLIO, by Ann Marie Barry

MARKETING CORPORATE IMAGE: THE COMPANY AS YOUR NUMBER ONE PRODUCT, by James R. Gregory with Jack G. Wiechmann

PROCTER & GAMBLE, by the Editors of Advertising Age

HOW TO BECOME AN ADVERTISING MAN, Second Edition, by James Webb Young

BUILDING YOUR ADVERTISING BUSINESS, Second Edition, by David M. Lockett

ADVERTISING & MARKETING CHECKLISTS, by Ron Kaatz

ADVERTISING MEDIA SOURCEBOOK, Third Edition, by Arnold M. Barban, Donald W. Jugenheimer, and Peter B. Turk

THE DIARY OF AN AD MAN, by James Webb Young

ADVERTISING COPYWRITING, Sixth Edition, by Philip Ward Burton

PROFESSIONAL ADVERTISING PHOTOGRAPHY, by Dave Saunders

DICTIONARY OF TRADE NAME ORIGINS, Revised Edition, by Adrian Room

For further information or a current catalog, write:
NTC Business Books
a division of *NTC Publishing Group*
4255 West Touhy Avenue
Lincolnwood, Illinois 60646-1975 U.S.A.